Rightsize Today to Create Your Best Life Tomorrow

A motivational guide for those seeking their ideal home later in life

Marni Jameson

Health Communications, Inc.
Boca Raton, Florida

www.hcibooks.com

Library of Congress Cataloging-in-Publication Data
is available through the Library of Congress

© 2024 Marni Jameson

ISBN-13: 978-07573-2484-0 (Paperback)
ISBN-10: 07573-2484-3 (Paperback)
ISBN-13: 978-07573-2485-7 (ePub)
ISBN-10: 07573-2485-1 (ePub)

All rights reserved. Printed in the United States of America. No part of this publication may be reproduced, stored in a retrieval system, or transmitted in any form or by any means, electronic, mechanical, photocopying, recording, or otherwise, without the written permission of the publisher.

HCI, its logos, and marks are trademarks of Health Communications, Inc.

Publisher: Health Communications, Inc.
301 Crawford Boulevard, Suite 200
Boca Raton, FL 33432-3762

Author photo ©Paige Nielson.
Cover, illustrations, interior design and formatting by Larissa Hise Henoch.

To DC,
who puts the heart in home.

CONTENTS

ACKNOWLEDGMENTS

When I started this book, I had just the seedling of an idea, the result of a question I wanted to answer for myself: How and where can I live my best life after sixty? I could foresee a lot of research ahead of me. What I could not foresee was just how many generous, thoughtful, and talented sources I would have the honor of meeting and working with along the way.

The fact that my idea has manifested itself into the pages you now hold is due in no small part to a tremendously dedicated team of professionals. I am so grateful for my agent Linda Konner, who talks me out of my bad ideas and into the good ones, including this book; for my editor Christine Belleris, who loved the concept from the start and who often shared her enthusiasm by sending encouraging e-mails like this one: "If your ears are constantly ringing it is because I have been telling so many people about this great project!" I wish to also thank Larissa Henoch for her stroke-of-genius cover graphic, and for staying up late many nights tending to every design detail; Mary Ellen Hettinger and Aldo Rosas for keeping their hands on the rudder of consistency; Lindsey Triebel Mach for promoting the book in so many creative ways, and the rest of the team at Health Communications, Inc.

For sharing their professional expertise, I am indebted to Joshua Becker, Bondi Coley, Wayne Edelman, Rich Eller, John Gartner, Gabe Geller, Kurt Gilbertson, Christopher Grubb, Lisa McManus, Heather Nickerson, Dawn O'Connor, Greg Owens, Nancy Patsios, Matt Paxton, Mary Helen Rogers, Andrew Rosen, Missy Tannen, and Jerry Weaver; and for sharing their research, Spencer High and Emily Thornton.

For their candor and for opening their homes and hearts to me, I thank Diane and Norm Bergan, the late Howard Bragman, Andy Fine, Bob Glockler, Liz Hicks, Chiqeeta and Craig Jameson, Paula and Paul Loftus, Jeannine and Don Maycott, Ann McGee, Katie and Thad Seymour, Jo Stewart, Bob Thacker and Karen Cherewatuk, and Suzanne White.

Finally, every book I write manages to engage my unwitting friends and family. For her eagle-eye proofreading and lifelong friendship, I thank Tracy Ramos. For a headshot that looks better than I deserve to, I thank my daughter Paige Nielson. And for reading and rereading, for listening and reframing, and for putting up with lots of late nights and lousy dinners, I thank the amazing Doug Carey (DC).

To all, I wish a long lifetime of soft pillows and sharp knives in the pitch-perfect place.

RIGHTSIZING—Moving to or creating a home that is the perfect physical, emotional, social, and financial fit for your life today and going forward. A rightsized home is neither too big nor too small; it's near what matters, and it contains only those items you need, use, and love.

Discover the Upside of Rightsizing

As someone who steeps herself in all things home, I've noticed something missing from the narrative. Something important. While much information is available for those buying their first homes, for those moving up and fixing up that four-square family home, and finally for those who can no longer live independently in their own homes, the literature is silent regarding one grand, glorious, and growing group. Overlooked are those older adults who have crossed or are about to cross what investors and analysts call the "freedom threshold."

I am one of them, which is why I began paying attention.

The freedom threshold is that turning point in life, usually around age sixty-one, plus or minus five years, when work and school no longer determine where we live. This means, my friends, we have a golden housing opportunity. That span of time between freedom and dependent living is lengthening as, collectively, we live longer, healthier lives than any generation before.

Those in this vital population include empty nesters, retirees, and those on the verge of these life transitions. Many, if not most, have a quarter of a century or more of living left. Because they no longer have to live by the schools their kids attended or near a job they had to commute to, they are free to live anywhere. They have a truly once-in-a-lifetime opportunity to choose where they want to live, in what type of housing, and with what belongings. They have a chance to realize what should be and could be the best years of their lives.

And many miss the boat.

Part of the reason they miss this golden opportunity is because, unlike those in other stages of life, many of these active older adults haven't been shown the way. Because the literature has ignored them, many haven't considered—let alone discovered—what is possible and better for them. If they do have a notion of what their dream life could be, they don't know how to get there. So they stay mired and rut bound in ill-suited, overfilled houses that hold them down and keep them from the richer, more joy-filled life that could be theirs.

I wrote this book to help those in this situation break free, to help those at this golden stage in life cross the bridge from stuck in the past to a lighter, less encumbered, more intentional future. I wrote it for all the cement-footed home dwellers out there—or those married to one—to help them realize that this golden age is their chance to design their next phase of life, to live where and how they want. I wrote it for those about to enter or who have already entered those sweet, free years after family and job responsibilities have lifted so we can make the most of them.

In the pages ahead, we'll journey through this rite of passage together. We'll break big questions into smaller ones and tackle them one at a time to find your answers: Should I stay in my home or move? If I move to a new place, should I stay in the same area or go somewhere new? What kind of housing would be ideal? What should I keep, let go of, and buy for my new rightsized life? We will dive into what matters to you, not your neighbor, into what you want from the rest of your life, and where to best find it, and we'll confront the roadblocks standing between where you are now and where you could be.

The journey begins in Part 1, where you will define what your rightsized life looks like. You'll do some soul-searching and complete a few exercises to divine your path. In Part 2, you'll find inspiration. Real people who have been where you are now, who changed up their housing when they hit their golden years and landed well, or occasionally stumbled and recovered. Whether they downsized, same-sized, upsized, or remodeled, they all reimagined and reevaluated their lives. They examined what was in them and what was missing, and then made intentional moves toward a better—and possibly their best—life.

Finally, in Part 3, we'll go room by room and explore what every rightsized home needs. You will learn to view belongings through a new lens, one that filters for what goes in your rightsized life, and what doesn't, so your new home is filled with quality, not clutter.

Come with me on this journey. Let's make the most of the life we have.

Part One

What Does Your Best Life Look Like?

It is only when we realize that life is taking us nowhere that it begins to have meaning.

—P.D. Ouspensky, Russian esotericist

Where do you live and why? Where *should you live and how? The questions merit asking. Hanging onto a home that no longer serves or suits us, or clinging to a residential status quo, is not a way to evolve into our best lives. Yet, we fear change.*

We fret. *What if I don't like my new home? What if it's worse, not better? What if I regret my decision? What if I make a big mistake? What if I don't want to sort through and purge my belongings? Sticking with the known, however impractical, can feel safer than trading it for the unknown. But at what cost? At the risk of missing out on the potential for greater joy and freedom that comes from intentionally living a rightsized life.*

Just ahead, we will explore what your rightsized life could look like, and what stands between you and a better way of life. Together, we'll cultivate courage.

CHAPTER 1

Finding the Fit—Creating a Vision

The kids are gone. You are retired or about to be. You no longer need to live close to their schools or your work. You've outgrown the house; that is, it's no longer a fit. Rooms go unused. The neighborhood isn't like it was. So why are you still there? I'm betting it's complacency. Or perhaps you're afraid of the unknown costs of buying a new place, including property taxes and the cost of the move itself. Moving means upheaval at every level—financial, emotional, social, psychological. It means going through all you own, facing lots of memories and, for that matter, your own mortality. It means dealing with uncertainty, a thousand decisions and hassles, and actual grief. Whether you are moving to a house that is smaller, similar in size, or larger but that offers more of what you want, you will still be closing a chapter of your life, which feels like loss.

And this is why many older adults remain tethered to homes that no longer suit them, maintaining more house than they need, using time, energy, and resources that they could spend on pursuits they enjoy more. (Would you rather pull weeds or travel?) Meanwhile, attics and garages, basements and back bedrooms become way stations and catchalls for so much yesterday, for the Scout uniforms, yearbooks, sports gear, unfinished needlepoint canvases, ancient paint cans, dime-store flower vases, and more, guaranteeing they will leave a big mess for those behind them.

So when those over a certain age—say, in the last third of life—are looking to downsize, clean house, and move all at the same time, many just say, "I'll just stay put, thank you very much."

It's not just their massive bedroom sets, armoires, hutches, and twelve-leaf dining-room tables holding them back but also the intangibles. Their memories, their family history, their identities are all in jeopardy, *or so they think.*

If you ask most older adults to get rid of a lifetime of acquired stuff and move from the large family house, where they raised the kids and hosted umpteen potlucks and as many pick-up ball games to a place that better suits their current lifestyle, financially, physically, and socially, and that is easier to maintain, they will tell you they would rather stand naked on the freeway.

And yet, that reluctance to lighten up, let go, and move on is often all that stands between them and a better life.

We can do this.

The Power of a Vision

You've probably heard the expression, be careful what you wish for. That is because most significant changes in our lives start with a vision. Dreams are powerful. For better or worse, we often attract, or some call it manifest, what we think about.

For instance, without dreams of the kind of person you want to be or marry, the kind of career you want to have, the kind of home you want to live in, the kind of friendships you want to develop and maintain, the places you want to go see, or the hobbies you want to pursue, you're destined to live by default, not by intention. You have a choice. You can either live your life like a piece of driftwood bobbing on a current, or a dandelion seed puff going where the wind blows you—or you can grab hold of your life by the steering wheel and take control.

Unless you make the effort to picture what could be and aim for that, you are destined to dwell in what is. Maybe that's fine. Or maybe you're missing out on a life that could be much better. For many people over the age of fifty-five, that best life is yet to come, but only if you pursue it with intention.

While I can't speak to the mysterious ways the world works, or to the role of divine intervention, I do believe, especially based on my experience, that we attract what we think about.

When I was approaching fifty, I was living in a large, beautiful home in the Colorado foothills of the Rocky Mountains, caring for my two daughters, who were in high school. Due to some significant financial reversals, the house was becoming unaffordable. It was 2010. We were in the depths of the recession. The market for large homes was nonexistent. Meanwhile, my twenty-year marriage was falling apart, and I was not earning much as a freelance journalist. I needed to get out from under the massive weight of the house and marriage and start earning more income.

I didn't know how I would get there, but I knew what I wanted. I wanted to rightsize my life, all of it: my home, my relationship, my career.

In December, my older daughter accepted an offer to attend a university in Texas, so she would be off. In January, I made a phone call to my editor at the *Los Angeles Times* and asked if she knew of any job openings. Three weeks later, I was interviewing at the *Orlando Sentinel*, a sister newspaper of the *L.A. Times*. I was offered the job of senior health reporter. During that interview, my then-husband got a call out of the blue from a real estate agent whom I had casually spoken to a few months earlier. The agent wondered if we might be willing to rent out our house. She had a couple that was interested. Indeed, they wanted to rent it for two years and buy much of the furniture.

Before I could accept the job or the rental offer, I had a few more problems to resolve. I needed to find decent housing in Florida and a good school for my younger daughter, a rising high school junior, who was coming with me. The housing I could afford on a journalist's salary, especially after what I'd been used to living in, was depressing. The day my younger daughter and I went to look at Orlando rental properties, the newspaper had a front-page story about a live-in, home-staging program. This company placed "property managers" in higher-end homes that were having trouble selling. In exchange for staging the houses to help them sell and accommodating showings, these managers got to live in these nice homes for a comparatively low monthly fee. I called. Though competition for these spots was stiff, I got the gig. Then a private school, which had no openings for rising juniors, got permission from its board to make a spot for my daughter.

The odds of all this happening were miniscule. Yet doors were opening. And they weren't done opening. My daughter going off to college had a horse that wasn't going to college. I couldn't take the horse with me, nor could I afford it any longer. The market for show horses was even worse than the market for high-end homes. I doubted I could find a buyer, but I put an ad online. Within a week, a veterinarian bought Hershey for the asking price, along with his horse tack and trailer.

Again, what are the chances?

The journalism job, the renters out of the blue, the live-in staging opportunity, the opening in the school, the horse buyer—all during a recession—I cleared hurdle after hurdle. I got out from under the pressures of a too-big house and a failing marriage. I got on my financial feet, got my career going again, and took care of my daughters. In all, I would live in and stage six homes in four years. (That's a lot of packing, purging, and perspiration!)

And the streak wasn't over. In 2014, I met a handsome widowed lawyer. We married in 2016 and settled in the Happy Yellow House.

Whether you attribute this unlikely series of events to faith, luck, manifestation, fate, or divine intervention, is up to you. All I know is it happened, and it was powerful. And it all started with a vision and the desire to make my life what I wanted.

Was it hard? Yes. Was it scary? Yes. Did everything work out? Amazingly. You just have to have faith.

For those who fear change, and my hand is up, having a vision of what you want can give you focus and direction and help you live your life with intention.

So let's dream for a minute. Let's imagine that you get one more shot at landing the ideal home for this golden time in your life. This home offers the perfect combination of location, size, furnishings, and affordability. It's near what and whom you love. It makes doing what you enjoy most—whether taking classes, fishing, volunteering, cooking, gardening, hiking, being with loved ones, going to the theater, or socializing—possible. It is the right physical and financial fit. It's neither too big nor too confining, and it supports you without your having to stress to support it. It's an easy keeper. And inside, you have only the belongings you need, use, and love—and no more. Your home has everything you need and enjoy and nothing you don't—no unnecessary stuff is weighing you down.

How does that feel?

Wonderful, right?

Get a pencil, and from the safety of your armchair we will conjure your next best place. The exercises at the end of this chapter will help you dial that in.

Think About What If, Not Why Not

Where in this wide world is your ideal home? What features does it have? How is it better than where you live now? What does it make possible for you? How is it furnished? How does it make you feel and why? If, after answering these questions, you come full circle and decide to stay right where you are because life couldn't get any better, fantastic! You are living with intention. But if you discover that your house, what's in it, and your surroundings are holding you back, let's fix that. Let's break through the inertia and create a path forward.

I like to define a rightsized home in three ways:

- It is in the right place.
- It is the right type of housing.
- It has just the right stuff.

Put more succinctly: place, dwelling, contents. As we go on this rightsizing journey, we will tackle these aspects to rightsizing and right living one at a time.

Before you pull up stakes, let's first ask: Why do you live where you live right now? Is it because you were born in this town or grew up there? Or did you wind up in this house because of a job, or for the schools? Are you here because this place was what you could afford at the time? Or maybe your answer is simply because it's your home.

Now ask: Would you choose this house and location if you were choosing again? Is it holding you back from a better life?

Lifestyle Inventory

Why do you live where you live right now?

_____

_____

_____

Would you choose this house and location if you were choosing again?

_____

_____

Is it holding you back from a better life?

_____

_____

Where Should I Live?

When considering where else might suit you better geographically—and it's okay if you have several locations in mind for now because you're dreaming—really dive in and ask what matters to you in terms of place.

Is it important that you live near family or friends? Or that you live in a place where you never have to shovel snow or drive on ice? Would you like to live somewhere that allows you to walk to good restaurants and shops? Is it important that the place is one you are familiar with, where you have a history and know your way around, or does the idea of living somewhere new appeal to you? Does your ideal place have an environment that nurtures you? Is it near water or meadows, farmland, or mountains? Does it have a community of likeminded people? Does it feed and engage you?

Note that these are just warm-up questions. Don't feel you need to provide definitive answers here. In Chapter 4, we will drill down further and actually (mathematically) determine your best place.

Where in this wide world is your ideal home? (Maybe more than one place?)

_____

_____

_____

_____

What features does it have?

_____

_____

How is it better than where you live now?

_____

_____

What does it make possible for you?

_____

_____

How is it furnished?

_____

_____

How does it make you feel and why?

_____

_____

CHAPTER 2

What Makes
People Move?

I have an affliction that has plagued me my whole life. Whenever I travel, whether to another city, state, or country, I look around at the people, the houses, the businesses, the ways of life, and say to myself, *Look at all the lives I am not living*. I want to try them all!

Now before you go thinking I'm one card short of a full deck, of course, I know we all get only one life. Most of the time I can barely manage the one I have, but I always wonder what it would be like to live in other places and what I am missing by not being there.

It's FOMO (fear of missing out) in the extreme.

Just visiting a place isn't enough. To know a place, to get under its skin, you have to live there. And, because most of us can only live in one place at a time, we need to choose carefully.

Where to live is one of those ginormous decisions, up there with: Should I marry this person? Is it time to start a family? Should I pursue this college major? Should I get a latte or cappuccino?

And because where we live is a life-defining choice, it raises questions. Specifically: How and why do people choose to live where they do? What makes them up and move to a new place? And when they do, are they generally happier? Is the grass greener?

At the core of most moves—whether to a house that is bigger or smaller, closer or farther from family, in or out of a city, less or more expensive, or in a warmer or colder climate—lies the hope that on the other side, life will be better.

I know there are exceptions, but generally, those who've decided to move believe that they are moving to a better situation, one where, if the wind blows just right, the quality of their life will tick up. Otherwise, why else would anyone dismantle a home and life, put all their worldly possessions in boxes and on trucks, and yank themselves like root-bound molars out of their communities? I mean, that's real grief.

Being obsessed with this notion of where we live and why, I paid close attention to a study that I came across that looked at how many Americans had moved in the past five years to a new state. The report combined US Census Bureau data with findings from a survey taken in September 2022 of 1,058 US adults.

Of those surveyed, more than one in four **(26 percent) had moved *to a new state* in the last five years,** according to the study commissioned by CraftJack, a company that connects professional contractors with those looking for them, the thought being that people on the move are often looking to do a home improvement.

That's a lot of U-Hauls. Moreover, of those who didn't move out of state in the past five years, 63 percent thought about it. Maybe you're one of them.

The survey also delved into the major reasons Americans moved to a new state. Because people often move for more than one reason, those who took the online survey were asked to check all that applied. Here are the leading reasons:

- Jobs (33 percent)
- To be closer to family (25 percent)—though 7 percent were moving away from family, and that's all I'm going to say about that
- For a lower cost of living (23 percent)
- To live in a new place (22 percent)
- To live in a warmer climate (13 percent)—though 6 percent wanted a colder climate
- Because ability to work remotely will let them live anywhere (9 percent)
- For a bigger home (7 percent)—though 4 percent were downsizing

Although these statistics factored in responses from adults of all ages, when adjusting the data to include only those fifty-five and up, the percentages didn't change much. Among Americans age fifty-five years or older, 23 percent had moved out of state in the last five years. Here were their top reasons:

- To be closer to family (17 percent)
- For a lower cost of living (16 percent)
- To live in a warmer climate (15 percent)
- To live in a new place (12 percent)
- To downsize (9 percent)

Among those age fifty-five and older who did not move out of state in the last five years, 59 percent had thought about doing so.

Rounding out the picture, a crunch of Census Bureau figures collected between April 2020 and July 2021 revealed the states most

Americans were moving to and from. Given that these data were taken during the height of the pandemic, researchers weren't surprised to see the trend out of big cities and south toward warmer climates or more outdoor life.

The top ten go-to states were Florida, Texas, Arizona, North Carolina, South Carolina, Tennessee, Georgia, Idaho, Utah, and Nevada.

Look Who's Moving

Even if you have no plans to leave your state or community, a look at the trends is telling:

- **Lifetime moves.** The average American moves 11.7 times in a lifetime, according to Census data. Those age fifty-five or older have already moved an average of nine times and have lived in three states.

- **Yearly moves.** In 2021, 8.4 percent of all US residents moved. Of those moves, 17.3 percent were to a new state, meaning nearly 5 million Americans left one state for another that year.

- **The cost.** The average move costs $3,946, according to the CraftJack survey. Of those who dream of living somewhere else, two-thirds (63 percent) said moving costs were holding them back.

- **Homebodies.** Not everyone has wanderlust: 63 percent of people currently live in the state where they grew up.

- **Happiness factor.** Perhaps the most interesting finding from this study was that 88 percent of those who moved out of state were happy they did.

In other words, if you're looking to move, you have plenty of company.

These statistics are just that. However, they are worth considering as you picture your own journey, which starts with the question: Should I move?

Downsizing Is Not a Demotion

Before we get back to you, let's address the elephant in the room: the fact that for some people, letting go of a large family home and moving somewhere smaller can feel like backsliding. This is especially true if you have been forced to give up a big, beautiful home because of a divorce, death, job loss, or other financial reversal. Then it can be a blow. I have been there. However, I also know from personal experience that when you have too much house, more house than you need, it's an albatross. Not only is it a waste of money, but it also drains your energy and time, resources you could be putting to better use.

I am not a proponent of living small. I am a proponent of living right. I like to approach rightsizing as if I were Goldilocks looking for the right fit: not too big, not too small, just right. The key is to find your fit. For those whose kids have grown and moved on, or whose households have fallen from five or four to two or one, often the best rightsizing move is to a smaller home. Regardless of how much sense it makes, this can still feel like a demotion. But let's look under the hood and ask why.

For most of their lives, Americans have focused on moving "up." Success has meant buying the bigger house to accommodate a growing family in a better neighborhood with better schools. Nothing wrong with that. The ability to afford and own a nice family home is a worthy goal and certainly an accomplishment. It tells the rest of the world "we've arrived." Even though this is such a big part of the American dream, this milestone can become a millstone.

Moving to a home that is smaller and a better fit is not a step back. You are in fact moving forward.

When we begin to reframe our move to a smaller home, whatever the circumstances, and see it not as downsizing or loss but as rightsizing and gain, the prospect stops feeling like a demotion and starts feeling like an accomplishment, a welcome evolution, a reward in its own right. As one downsizer we will meet in Chapter 9 put it, "I feel like I lost weight." You no longer have to shoulder more house than you need.

Indeed, the quality of life for rightsizers often goes up when they have to care for no more house or yard than they need or want. Rightsizing frequently frees up capital, allowing older adults to enjoy more of what they love. For those who want to travel, locking up and leaving town becomes much easier. Finally, once rightsizers have done the hard work of purging and cleaning house, and reducing their footprint—which, I will stress, you should do no matter how big or small your home is—they will be giving their heirs an enormous gift. Can I get an "Amen"?

More Seniors, Same-Size

On the flip side, some come to a point where they want, and finally can afford, more house because they want to have all the kids, their spouses, and grandkids over. That's a wonderful insight and accomplishment, too. Choosing to same-size or upsize is more common than you might think.

"One of the persistent myths we have about retirees is that they want to downsize, but that's not true today," said Dr. Jessica Lautz, an economist and one of the lead researchers behind the National Association of Realtors' 2023 Home Buyers and Sellers Generational

Trends Report. Among those between the ages of fifty-eight and seventy-six who bought homes last year, most were same-sizing. Nearly one in five bought homes over 3,000 square feet.

To create the report, Lautz and other researchers analyzed responses from nearly 5,000 US homeowners who bought and sold homes in the previous year. The report found several more trends you may find promising. These were the findings among older buyers, which they break into three groups: younger baby boomers, age fifty-eight to sixty-seven; older baby boomers, age sixty-eight to seventy-six; and the silent generation, age seventy-seven to ninety-seven. Here are their findings:

- **Same-sizing.** Among home buyers between the ages of fifty-eight and seventy-six, most bought homes that were the same size as the home they sold.
- **Weighty demographic.** Of all US home buyers, 43 percent are fifty-eight or older.
- **The sweet spot.** Over half of home buyers over age fifty-eight bought a home between 1,501 and 2,500 square feet. However, 17 percent of younger boomers, 19 percent of older boomers, and 13 percent of the silent generation bought homes over 3,000 square feet.
- **Houses, not condos.** Among those buyers fifty-eight and older, three-fourths bought single-family homes.
- **Independent living.** Only 7 percent of all buyers over sixty bought housing in senior communities. "That number really speaks to the decline seen in older buyers seeking senior-related housing," Lautz said. "It seems today's seniors increasingly want to live independently."

- **Bargaining power.** Older homeowners often have accrued significant assets, including a tremendous amount of home equity, so they are holding the cards. "They are cash heavy and often come to the table with no contingencies, so in the case of a bidding war, they will win," Lautz said. Among younger boomers, 43 percent paid all cash for their home, and among older boomers, 51 percent did, compared with only 7 percent of those ages thirty-three to forty-two.

Age has its privileges.

Now back to you. Let's do a deeper dive into where your best place is.

> Of those who moved out of state, 88 percent surveyed were happy that they did.

Checklist: How to Know When It's Time to Move

- ☐ You have more house than you need or want to take care of.
- ☐ You don't have enough house to accommodate your family or friends when they visit, and you'd like to.
- ☐ As a retired empty nester, you have better places to be than where you live.
- ☐ You dream of selling your main house, using the equity to buy a smaller house, and using any remaining profit to enhance your retirement.
- ☐ You would like to cash in your big house and buy two small ones.
- ☐ You really want a small place as a landing pad between trips you plan to take.
- ☐ You would prefer less yard to maintain.

☐ You want to age in place, and certain features of the home, such as stairs, won't allow that.

☐ You want to live closer to family.

☐ The neighborhood is full of young families, and you've aged out.

☐ Your family and close friends are no longer nearby.

☐ The only reason you live in this house is for the quality of the schools your kids no longer attend, or for a job you no longer commute to.

☐ You can't bear the thought of spending one more winter (or summer) where you live.

☐ Your house has appreciated nicely and could buy you more of what you want somewhere else.

☐ Other aspects of the neighborhood have changed for the worse, perhaps there is more crime or congestion.

Based on a review of your answers, check one of the following:
☐ **Stay** ☐ **Go**

What Do I Want in a Place to Live?

In terms of location, check all that are important to you.
It is important that my next home . . .

☐ Is close to family.

☐ Has a warm climate year-round.

☐ Has seasons.

☐ Is in a town with an affordable cost of living.

☐ Is close to restaurants, shops, theater, and other cultural opportunities.

☐ Has a view of, or is near, mountains, water, meadows, farmland, city life.

☐ Is close to a college or place where I can take adult education classes.

☐ Is close to excellent health care.

☐ Offers the access to church, clubs, or civic or educational opportunities I enjoy.

☐ Other

_____

_____

_____

Given the above, I could see myself living in the following cities:

_____

_____

_____

_____

_____

_____

What Do I Want in a House?

Once you decide where to live, and that answer may be evolving, the next question is, In what type of housing? Again, you might be living in the perfect home, but let's be sure. Are there rooms you never or rarely use? Are you spending more time and money on your home than you would like to maintain it? What features does your ideal home have? Many adults at this stage of life want more freedom and fun and less responsibility. They want a smaller home that they can lock up and leave while they travel. They don't want to maintain a yard or pay for utilities in a wing of the house they never use. They may still want a guest room but don't need to house four kids. Others want to be the landing pad for all the kids and grandkids, so they size up so their home can be the hub of the family. Maybe this is when they finally get their gourmet kitchen, paint or yoga studio, workshop, and herb garden. What do you dream of doing at home? How do you dream of living?

I could see myself living in (check all that apply):

☐ A single-family home

☐ A townhome or condo

☐ A cottage

☐ A cabin

☐ An apartment

☐ A fifty-five-plus community

☐ A guest house near my kids

I would like my next house to have:

☐ Less than 1,000 square feet

☐ 1,000–2,000 square feet

☐ 2,000–3,000 square feet

☐ More than 3,000 square feet

☐ A main bedroom suite on the main floor

- ☐ One story

- ☐ Two stories

- ☐ One bedroom

- ☐ Two bedrooms

- ☐ Three or more bedrooms

- ☐ A guest room

- ☐ A garage

- ☐ A view of _____

- ☐ A great kitchen

- ☐ Less yard

- ☐ More yard

- ☐ Walkability to restaurants and shops

- ☐ Lower overhead, as in lower utility bills and taxes

- ☐ Fewer expenses overall

What else?

_____

_____

_____

_____

_____

_____

CHAPTER 3

Should I Stay or Should I Go?

Many of you know that catchy song "Should I Stay or Should I Go?" by the English punk rock band The Clash.

The song, which debuted in 1982, expresses the ambivalence of a lover wondering if he should stay in a relationship or leave. The song resonates with those who have a foot in the house where they live, the place they know, and who are dipping a toe in another place they're thinking about living. It speaks to those struggling to decide whether they should stay in the home they have or move to one that might be a better fit.

It certainly seemed to be Andy Fine's theme song.

As I started writing this book, Andy Fine, a reader who had been following my home column in *The Mercury News*, sent me an e-mail.

Unbeknownst to him, he was asking the very questions I was endeavoring to address:

Dear Marni,

I've recently begun reading your columns. I don't know if you answer personal questions, but I hope so! I'm seventy-five, and no, I don't believe it. I live in Northern California, in a 3,000-square-foot house. My current house is way too big to keep up with. I'm thinking of selling it in the next year or two and downsizing big-time. I know that means getting rid of a lot of things, which I've never done.

The first question is, Where? I like my area. However, I'm also thinking of moving to the same Midwest town where my son, his wife, and my two young granddaughters, ages three and five, live. I can see living there. I go back annually for the holidays. However, the winters are frigid. Some days the high has a minus sign in front of it. I'm also not positive that they'd want me there. I get along well with them, but how can one truly know. If I ask, they'd likely say, "Sure, Dad," but would they really mean it?

I recognize that with aging there are potential problems to living alone, should something adverse happen to me health-wise. With my son and his wife working full-time and raising two daughters, they're not going to have much free time. While I don't expect them to take care of me, or to move in with them, if something were to happen, it would be better to have responsible, younger family in the same town.

The second question is, Move to what? A smaller house, a condo or townhouse, or a senior fifty-five-plus living community? I don't want a yard to take care of anymore, though I know one could hire a gardener. I realize with a townhouse or condo, one can have neighbors who are much closer than in a house, which can be good or bad.

Third question, How does one downsize? Going from 3,000 square feet to, say, 1,500 to 1,700 square feet means getting rid of lots of stuff, which I've never done before. Dining room table and chairs? Curio cabinets with some of my beloved parents' antiques? Extra bedroom sets? Kids' stuff that's still here? And so on . . .

I'd deeply appreciate any help you can give.

In short, he was asking exactly the questions I was writing about: Where? In what? With what?

Since he had pretty much thrown a pitch right over the heart of the plate, I reached out to Andy with this offer: I would help him through this process if he would be candid, work with me to apply my rightsizing methods, and let me use his example in my book.

He willingly accepted.

We spoke on the phone over the next month, for an hour or two at times, and exchanged more e-mails.

I learned this.

Andy has lived in the East Bay, an hour outside San Francisco, for twenty-four years. Divorced for thirty years, he never remarried. He has two adult children. He retired in 2001 from a career in financial services, mostly as a bond portfolio manager. Though financially comfortable, he's suffered a couple of financial setbacks, so he does not consider himself wealthy. "It's not like I have a couple million in the bank, but I have no major financial problems," he said.

He describes himself as "frugal by nature. I rarely go out to eat." He lives off Social Security, which he started taking at age sixty-two, some real estate investments, and a couple of annuities. Financial reasons aren't driving his desire to downsize and move.

He's weighing his options, which include staying in the Bay Area, but in different housing, or moving out of state. Among the places he is considering are Cedar Rapids, Iowa, where his son lives with his wife and two children, and Falls Church, Virginia, where his daughter, who is single with no children, lives. He has a good relationship with them both.

He also is on good terms with his ex-wife, who lives near their son. "As far as I know, we get along," he said. She is remarried. Andy has one sibling, a brother he is close to, who lives in Punta Gorda, Florida, a fourth place he's considering.

He doesn't care much for the arts, clubs, or social scenes. What he does love to do is read and play bridge. "I spend half my day reading, and eight to ten hours a week playing duplicate bridge, which I'm passionate about."

Though generally healthy, he has battled cancer twice and took a fall last year and broke his femur. "I've had a few wake-up calls reminding me that I'm not immortal. These health scares have kind of forced my hand and sped up my desire to relocate. I want to be proactive and make a move before I have to."

Though the need to move is clear, the thought of it is overwhelming. "The decisions are paralyzing me," he wrote.

The first question in our decision tree, whether to leave his current house, was easy to answer: "I've never loved everything about this house and have no desire to live in a house this big," he said. "I don't need it. It's full of so many things I haven't used in many years."

He ticks off some of them: eight work suits and forty to fifty ties. "I haven't worn a suit in years. I have hundreds of books I won't read again, a dining room table and chairs not used in years. I have no interest in hosting dinner parties."

He also has no desire to take care of a yard. "I do a lousy job of caring for it because it's not my thing. I'm not Mr. Green Jeans," he said.

"In short, I don't want to stay here. It's too much house to maintain. I'd rather spend time playing bridge and reading."

Because it saddens me to think that he's been retired for over twenty years and living in a house he doesn't love that isn't near family, I feel an urgency to help him move on to a place, to a home that's a better fit, and a life that is more fulfilling.

He agrees, selling the two-story house and moving is a given. The question now is where to move. "In theory I could move anywhere," he said. We bat around options and narrow the list to these four, for the following reasons:

- **San Francisco Bay Area.** He lists his familiarity with the area, the good weather, and having very good medical care close by as the three main positives. While he knows people who live nearby, he has no family there and no one he is close with. Plus it's expensive.

- **Cedar Rapids, Iowa.** The upside of moving here would be getting to watch his granddaughters grow up and being close to family, which could be helpful if he had any health issues. The area has a low cost of living, low crime, and nice people, but harsh winters.

- **Falls Church, Virginia.** In addition to his daughter, Andy's best friend since the first grade lives in the area, which is just outside Washington, DC. However, the high cost of housing and cold winters turn him off.

- **Punta Gorda, Florida.** The plusses of this location are he could spend time with his brother and would have access to good medical care. While the cost of living would be more than Iowa's, it would be less than Virginia's or California's. The downsides are humidity and hurricanes.

The Decision Tree, Weighing the Variables

We ran the options through the decision tree, which you'll learn about shortly, to find the optimal place for his rightsizing journey. But before we sort through Andy's decision tree, let's work on yours.

The reason deciding whether and where to move is so overwhelming is because it involves many factors. However, the decision gets easier when you break it down into a string of decisions.

Answer these questions for yourself. If you'll be moving with a spouse or partner, have your mate answer these questions, too. Because everyone's situation is different, the right rightsizing answer for you won't be the same for someone else.

Stay-or-Go Decision Tree

Should you stay in your house or go? (Refer to your "How to Know When It's Time to Move" checklist in Chapter 2.)

⇨ **IF YOU STAY** in your home, what modifications would you need to make so your home fits your lifestyle and allows you to age in place?

    ⇨ **Ruthlessly sort** through and assess all you own: toss, donate, sell, keep.

⇨ **IF YOU GO,** where to?

    ⇨ **Same community**, but other housing?

        ⇨ **What type** of housing?

            ⇨ **Ruthlessly sort** through and assess all you own: toss, donate, sell, keep.

    ⇨ **New city**

        ⇨ **Which city?** (Use weighted average exercise in the next section to decide.)

            ⇨ **What type** of housing?

                ⇨ **Ruthlessly sort** through and assess all you own: toss, donate, sell, keep.

STAY	GO	
⇩ In current home remodel or retrofit to rightsize	⇩ To new home in same community	⇩ To new home in new community
⇩ Purge	⇩ Type of housing?	⇩ What city?
	⇩ Purge	⇩ Type of housing?
		⇩ Purge

Andy has affirmed one key decision. He will move. Now he must decide whether to stay in the Bay Area or move somewhere new. We'll find out his best place in the next chapter.

CHAPTER 4

How to Know If the Grass Is Greener—Do the Math

Every year, many organizations come out with their "best places to retire" list. Others post cost-of-living indexes, ranking states from most affordable to most expensive. These tools offer interesting, if not always consistent, reference points. However, they only provide a piece of the puzzle. Missing from these rankings is what matters to *you*.

The question of "Where should I live?" is difficult because it involves many highly personal variables, such as closeness to family, cost of living, climate, community, access to what you enjoy, and more. Only you can weigh how important each of those variables is to you. For instance, if being near family is high on your priority list, you won't find that baked into any generic "best places to retire" list.

Only you can decide your best place.

In the previous chapter, we determined that for Andy, rightsizing would mean moving out of his too-big home. The question now is, move where? If you know the house you're in is no longer right, is the grass greener somewhere else, or should you just resize and stay in the town where you live?

To figure out which of his four options would best fit his rightsizing goals, I asked Andy what he wanted from a place. What did he value? I had him rank the following variables on a scale of one to five, one being not important and five being extremely important.

Go ahead. Answer these for yourself, too:

Where-to-Live Values Survey

What Matters?

On a 1–5 scale, rate how important the following are to you.

_____ **Proximity to family.** This could also include the importance of being near dear, close friends or loved ones who are like family.

_____ **Weather.** How important is it to live in a place that has the kind of climate you want, whether that's year-round sunshine or seasons with snow?

_____ **Familiarity with the area.** How important is it to you that you know your way around a place and feel at home there? A ranking of five would mean that knowing a place is extremely important and that you do not like the idea of living in unfamiliar territory. A ranking of one means you don't mind getting to know a new place, and the thought of learning about a new town actually interests you.

_____ **Cost of living.** How important is it to you that a city is affordable with regard to cost of housing, taxes, and general living expenses? A score of five indicates that the cost of living in a city or its affordability is extremely important to you.

_____ **Proximity to good health care.** How important is it that you are close to good hospitals?

_____ **Proximity to education and culture.** How important is it that you are near theaters, museums, good restaurants, the symphony, ballet, and a university or other education center that offers enrichment, such as adult education classes?

_____ **Proximity to social activities.** How important is it to you that you have easy access to a place of worship, clubs, and organized recreation that you enjoy? A five would indicate extremely important.

What else? While this list is fairly comprehensive, other factors may be important to you, so add them. For instance, perhaps you value access to public transportation, being close to a major airport, or living in a state that aligns with your political beliefs. Customize this list for you.

_____

_____

_____

_____

Here's how Andy ranked these factors:

- Proximity to family: 4
- Weather: 4
- Familiarity with the area: 3

- Cost of living: 3
- Proximity to good health care: 5
- Proximity to education and culture: 1
- Proximity to social activities: 1

Now comes the real test. I had Andy rate, again on a one-to-five scale, how each of the areas he was considering moving to measured up in each of these categories. That is, how did he perceive that these cities fared with regard to weather, cost of living, access to health care, and so on? Once he did that, we could combine the importance of each of these variables along with how he ranked them to calculate a weighted average. This would reveal the location that would deliver the most of what he wanted. You'll see. You do the exercise, too.

Rate Your Places

On a 1–5 scale, rate how well each of the cities you are considering measures up in each category. Answer the following set of questions for as many places as you are considering.

List your potential places:

_____

_____

_____

_____

_____

How does (fill in the location) rate in the following categories:

_____ It is close to family or good friends.

_____ I like the weather there.

_____ I know the area well.

_____ The cost of living is affordable.

_____ Good health care is available.

_____ I would have easy access to education and culture.

_____ It would be easy to access social, religious, or recreational activities I enjoy.

What else? How does this location measure up in terms of what else matters to you?

_____

_____

_____

_____

Here are Andy's answers:

California

Proximity to family: 1

Weather: 4

Familiarity with area: 4

Cost of living: 1

Health care: 5

Education and culture: 5

Social activities: 4

Iowa

Proximity to family: 4

Weather: 2

Familiarity with area: 3

Cost of living: 5

Health care: 4

Education and culture: 3

Social activities: 3

Virginia
Proximity to family: 4
Weather: 3
Familiarity with area: 1
Cost of living: 1
Health care: 5
Education and culture: 5
Social activities: 5

Florida
Proximity to family: 4
Weather: 4
Familiarity with area: 1
Cost of living: 3
Health care: 4
Education and culture: 3
Social activities: 3

We're not done yet! With those scores, we can now calculate a weighted average. (Trust me, I am no math wizard, but this is not as complicated as it sounds.) Here's how. Each variable has a different level of importance—in Andy's case being near family ranks higher (4) than being near social activities (1). So by using the importance rating as a multiplier and multiplying it by how each location ranks in that category, we can get a fuller picture of how each city stacks up overall.

Here's the beauty of this math. When mentally comparing places, holding all these variables in your mind at once gets unwieldy and only grows more complicated when comparing several cities. This calculation does that for you.

Stay with me. If proximity to family ranks a four in overall in importance, as it does for Andy, and actual proximity to family in a city or state, say the Bay Area, rates a two, then we multiply four times two and get eight points for the family variable in California. In Iowa, where proximity to family measures a four, the value is sixteen (four times four).

Likewise, if weather ranks a four out of five in overall importance, and the weather in Iowa rates a two, the total value of weather in Iowa would be eight (four times two), whereas in California, where weather rates a four, the value is sixteen (four times four).

Here's how it played out:

Importance Overall		California	Iowa	Virginia	Florida
Proximity to family:	4	1/4	4/16	4/16	4/16
Weather:	4	4/16	2/8	3/12	4/16
Familiarity:	3	4/12	3/9	1/3	1/3
Cost of living:	3	1/3	5/15	1/3	3/9
Health care:	5	5/25	4/20	5/25	4/20
Education, culture:	1	5/5	3/3	5/5	3/3
Social activities:	1	4/4	3/3	5/5	3/3
Sum		24/69	24/74	24/69	22/70

If your numbers are accurate, the results should point you in the right direction.

In his case, Iowa, with a score of 74, won. Note that even though California and Virginia had the same raw score as Iowa, of 24, that number would only put California or Virginia ahead if all factors were equal, which they're not.

Where Should You Live?

Now let's see how your potential places measure up. Remember to tailor your list by adding variables that matter to you. If you are making this decision along with your spouse, have each of you fill in the blanks separately, and then compare results.

In the first column on the left, enter how you rank each category as you did before. Then, under each city, to the left of the slash, enter how that city ranks in each category. Then multiply that number by the overall importance and enter the product to the right of the slash.

Now add up both columns. The sum on the left of your slash marks is your raw score. This is how a city would measure up if all variables were equally important, but they're not. The sum on the right is the weighted average, how that city measures up based on what you value.

Find Your Match

	Importance Overall	Current City	Optional City #1	Optional City #2
Proximity to family:		/	/	/
Weather:		/	/	/
Familiarity with area:		/	/	/
Cost of living:		/	/	/
Health care:		/	/	/
Education, culture:		/	/	/
Social activities:		/	/	/
Sum		/	/	/

Surprised? Most people find that the data confirm what their gut has been saying, only now they have the numbers to prove it. But that's not always the case.

Craig and Chiqeeta

As I write this, my older brother and his wife are in the throes of this tumultuous decision. Craig and Chiqeeta, who have had long productive careers and no children, are on the verge of retiring. He's sixty-six and she's sixty-seven. They are looking to leave Los Angeles, the city they have called home for more than thirty years. Craig has lived in Southern California his whole life. Chiqeeta grew up in Illinois. It's obvious to those who know them that this will be a beneficial move, but they're anxious.

As part of their exit strategy, they sold their townhome when the market was peaking, to get liquidity. They also sold a cabin they had built in Northern California, after ruling it out as a retirement home. (Course correction is critical.) They have the money set aside to buy a single-family home somewhere outside California. They are looking for a three-bedroom house with around 2,500 square feet. Meanwhile, they are renting a two-bedroom apartment.

They know they want to move away from the urban density and the high cost of living that is part of life in Los Angeles. They have even picked out a city, Midland, Michigan, where they would like to retire. The town is both affordable and near family. Chiqeeta's older sister and her husband live there, and their son, his wife, and two boys. They have visited often and have looked at houses. They can easily afford a single-family home with a yard for their dog, Charlie, and a studio for Craig to draw and play guitar, his two favorite pastimes. They can experience four seasons, which they don't get in Southern California, and their money will go a lot farther.

As publisher of a city magazine, Chiqeeta is in the mix and has a great connection with her community, but she's ready to move and has no reservations. She wants a simpler life. "I want to walk down the street and have coffee with a neighbor."

Craig, on the other hand, has lead shoes. He's reluctant to leave the architecture practice he has built over thirty years. The question of "Who will I be when I'm not a Los Angeles architect with my own firm?" gnaws at him. We don't know, do we? He does know he's tired of practicing architecture and of the demands that come with running a firm. He has a partner who can take the reins. But still, there's that scary crossover, when you go from earning an income to drawing from your retirement. How's that going to work out? Will it?

Like so many standing on this threshold, Craig is afraid of trading the known for the unknown. Every time I talk to them, they are in a different place. Sometimes they've taken a few steps forward, others a giant step back. The timeline shifts. They often disagree.

Sound familiar?

They are squarely on my mind as I write this book. Their fear of leaving the known for the unknown, regardless of how much sense it makes on paper, is profound, and valid. Thus, with them in my sights, I hope to motivate, explore, guide, encourage, and shine a light on the path forward.

Though Craig and Chiqeeta have decided to move from Los Angeles to Midland, Michigan, just for fun I had them take the Where-to-Live Values Survey. In addition to comparing Michigan to their current home in Los Angeles, I (selfishly) and for the sake of comparison added Central Florida, where I live, and Colorado where my oldest daughter (their niece) and her husband have settled, to see whether one of these other places would be a better fit.

The results are telling.

Craig's Results

	Importance Overall	Los Angeles California	Midland Michigan	Orlando Florida	Denver Colorado
Proximity to family:	4	1/4	4/16	5/20	3/12
Weather:	3	5/15	2/6	3/9	3/9
Familiarity with area:	2	5/10	3/6	1/2	2/4
Cost of living:*	5	1/5	5/25	3/15	2/10
Health care:	5	5/25	5/25	5/25	5/25
Education, culture:	5	5/25	3/15	5/25	4/20
Social activities:	5	3/15	3/15	5/25	3/15
OTHER Public services:	4	4/16	5/20	4/16	4/16
Sum		29/115	30/128	31/137	26/111

*Many cost-of-living indexes are available, which you can refer to when assessing what it would cost to live in various parts of the country. A 2023 survey from World Population Review ranked cost of living by state. In this survey, for instance, out of 50 states (with the 50th ranked being the most expensive), Michigan ranked 14th, Florida 27th, Colorado 34th, and California 47th. (See Resources in the back of the book).

Chiqeeta's Results

	Importance Overall	Los Angeles California	Midland Michigan	Orlando Florida	Denver Colorado
Proximity to family:	4	1/4	4/16	4/16	1/4
Weather:	3	5/15	4/12	3/9	4/12
Familiarity with area:	1	5/5	3/3	1/1	1/1
Cost of living:*	5	1/5	5/25	5/25	3/15
Health care:	5	5/25	4/20	5/25	4/20
Education, culture:	4	5/20	4/16	3/12	3/12
Social activities:	4	5/20	4/16	4/16	4/16
OTHER Shopping:	5	5/25	3/15	4/20	3/15
Sum		32/119	31/123	29/124	23/95

Having couples take the survey separately is important, as it allows them to consider what matters to their partner and also to see where they align and don't. It also opens the way to productive conversations.

The results above illustrate the importance of looking at weighted averages as opposed to raw scores. If you looked at just the raw scores, three of the cities (Los Angeles, Midland, and Orlando) rank pretty closely. Scores range from 29 to 32. Not until you factor in what each individual values in a place do the better candidates surface, while the poorer options recede.

In their case, the numbers show the need to leave California is clear, and they should take Colorado off the list. Florida ekes out a win over Michigan, but Midland is still a far cry better than where they are. The point is, the exercise isn't a definite answer but a divining rod to guide you. When I last checked in with them, they had agreed on a hard stop date six months out. By that date, they will leave their respective jobs and Los Angeles and head to the Great Lakes State to begin their next adventure.

CHAPTER 5

What If the Plan Backfires?

Not everyone who rightsizes sticks the landing the first time, as the following rightsizers will tell you.

Shortly after hearing me speak at a senior life conference, where I asked the audience to think about what they valued and how they wanted to spend the rest of their lives, Liz Hicks reached out to tell me about her rightsizing journey, one she still feels she hasn't gotten quite right—but she's getting warmer.

Of course, I was intrigued. I'm just as interested in learning from those who make mistakes as I am from those who get it right the first time.

A career engineer, Liz had to reengineer her own life after her divorce in 2014. She moved out of her five-bedroom house on five acres in Colorado into a two-bedroom apartment nearby.

"While downsizing was hard," she said, "because you're shaking up everything you worked so hard to establish, getting rid of a lot of stuff also felt good. You just don't need it. The move made my life simpler, and, because I scaled back, I was better off financially."

She let family and friends take what they wanted and then donated the rest. (Key point: she did not pay to store it!) "Everything I gave up was all totally replaceable, and besides, stuff accumulates faster than you want it to," she said.

She stayed in Colorado until her son and only child finished college there, then, sick of the cold, she arranged for a job transfer with her company to her favorite vacation spot: Florida. In 2020, at age fifty, she moved to the Sunshine State.

Soon after she arrived, she bought what she described as "a beautiful 3,000-square-foot executive forever home."

A few years later, she tells me she's not sure it was the best move, especially now that she's looking at retiring in a couple of years. "I'm sitting in this lovely home thinking, *This is just too much*," she said. "The house is more of a burden than a blessing. I don't want to go into retirement feeling tired. The house is expensive to maintain, and the area is busier than where I want to ultimately retire."

So, what happened? She did everything right. She downsized and then rightsized. She thought about where and how she wanted to live. She was familiar with the place she was heading and picked it intentionally.

But something did happen that put everything in a new light: kidney cancer. Fortunately, the doctors caught it early, and today Liz is cancer free. But she views the world through a different lens.

"When I got the cancer card, I realized the last thing I wanted to spend my time on was taking care of a house. For me, no house is worth the amount of time I spend on this one. If it's not the roof, it's the air conditioning. The problem is not so much the money but the time. And where I spend my time and focus is now top of mind. Time for friends and family instantly became much more important than a house or the things in it.

"After my diagnosis, I started asking, *How do I spend my days, what am I spending my energy on? Am I where I want to be and doing what I want to do?*"

Liz may not have the answers, but she's certainly asking the right questions.

As she searches for that next rightsized house, she pictures a home about half the size of what she has, say 1,500 to 1,700 square feet. "But there's more to a home than square feet," she said. "I'm interested in the social aspect. I would love to walk out the door and be in a community where I could walk to dinner and the grocery store.

"I will be paying attention to how my decision will affect my time, which I want to spend with my family, my friends, my church, taking more trips, and doing what I love. That to me is living."

Her plan between now and when she retires is to take vacations in towns that interest her. "I'm thinking of moving to the Carolinas," she said. First stop is Greenville, South Carolina.

Out of curiosity, I suggested Liz take the Where-to-Live Values Survey and compare her hypothetical dream town of Greenville and her current town of Oviedo, Florida. The exercise appealed to her engineering side. She tailored the list to include a few more factors that were important to her, such as pace of the town, access to hiking trails, and proximity to the ocean.

	Importance Overall	Oviedo Florida	Greenville South Carolina
Proximity to family:	2	3/6	2/4
Weather:	5	4/20	3/15
Familiarity with area:	1	4/4	2/2
Cost of living:*	5	2/10	4/20
Health care:	5	5/25	4/20
Education, culture:	5	4/20	3/15
Social/church activities:	5	5/25	4/20
Pace of town:	4	2/8	3/12
Proximity to beach:	4	3/12	2/8
Access to hiking trails:	5	3/15	4/20
Walkability:	4	2/8	4/16
Sum		37/153	35/152

Interestingly, the scores of her current town and her dream town were neck and neck.

"That's not a big enough improvement in lifestyle to know it would be a great change," she said when I shared her results. Now she's rethinking her plan. "It's making me think I need to keep looking around. I don't want change for the sake of change."

Maybe the grass isn't greener.

"It makes me wonder whether I'm not focusing enough on the good of what I have. If what I really want is less house, and a more walkable neighborhood, maybe that can happen here."

And that's exactly what this exercise is meant to do—make you think.

Too Much of a Good Thing

When the time came for Jo and Jim Stewart to retire from their high-octane jobs, they knew just the place. Whenever the Washington, DC, power couple—Jim was a CBS news correspondent and Jo worked in commercial lending—needed some down time, they headed for Destin, Florida, a quiet, beautiful beach town in Florida's panhandle.

> We had to get it wrong to get it right.
>
> —Jo Stewart

They liked the town so much they bought a vacation home there. They retired when Jo was fifty-five and Jim was sixty-three, sold their DC home, and moved to Destin "for good." They moved into their vacation home and moved Jim's ninety-year-old mother into a senior living center nearby. Then they set to work building their dream house.

"Everything was falling into place," Jo said. There was just one problem. They were bored. "Destin was a great place to relax, unwind, and escape from the rat race, but once we lived there full-time, we realized it was a little too quiet."

They yearned for a bit more culture, live theater, good restaurants, shops, and museums. When they accepted the fact that they had retired in a place that ultimately wasn't where they wanted to be, they made a course correction—carefully.

To find their happy place, Jo used a search tool available through her real estate connections. The tool lets you explore not just cities but neighborhoods to find out what the residents are like in terms of age, education, and political party.

Their search led them to Winter Park, Florida, which checked all their boxes. It had the right blend of small-town vibe and chic shops, arts and culture, and a neighborhood where they fit in. When Jim's mom passed at age 100, they left Destin and bought a home in Winter Park, which they renovated and where they plan to stay.

Today, Jo helps fundraise for the Orlando Museum of Art, volunteers at the botanical gardens, and takes oil painting classes. "It's all within reach and more," she said, adding, "We had to get it wrong to get it right."

Beware the Vacation Effect

Both Liz Hicks and Jo Stewart also issued this word of caution. Although vacationing in a place is a good way to get to know it, don't forget, life isn't a vacation.

"I quickly learned that what I loved about going to Florida was staying in a full-service resort on the beach," Liz said. "But once I moved here, there was no cabana boy bringing me a towel and a drink."

Similarly, Jo said, "When we would come to Destin after a hectic time at work, we would put our toes in the sand and all our worries melted away. But ultimately, you want more."

CHAPTER 6

But My Stuff Is in the Way

Knowing what you should do and doing it are as close as third cousins twice removed: related but leagues apart. Though Andy Fine now knows what he wants to do, he has to unpack a 3,000-square-foot house he has filled up over the last twenty-four years.

My brother and his wife need to separate and disentangle themselves from their work lives, work through a storage facility of stuff above and beyond what they have in their home, and deal with finding a new home in an unfamiliar state. It's enough to make anyone just say, "Forget it, I'll stay put."

The inertia of stuff and circumstances is a hurdle Realtors know well. Some have asked me for help.

"What can I say to senior sellers to help them move?" This question came in an e-mail from a Realtor sharing his lament. He'd recently worked with several families where the adult children of senior parents were stuck unloading a house that their parents had left in a mess.

> Neglected, cluttered houses sell for on average $50,000 to $60,000 less than they would if they were cleared out and cleaned up.
>
> —Jerry Weaver, Realtor

This was also me ten years earlier, cleaning out my parents' home of nearly half a century. Frankly, I needed a backhoe and a bottle of spirits.

"In a typical scenario," wrote Jerry Weaver, the Realtor, from Novi, Michigan, "the daughter calls. Dad has died, and Mom has moved to a condo or retirement home. The house she's moved out of is full of stuff. The finances are in turmoil because Dad handled all that. And Mom needs all the money she can get out of her home."

He wanted to know if I had any tips. (I'm sharing this, so you know what a mess you will leave your loved ones if you don't deal with your stuff—not just once, but regularly.)

"I like to believe I am very good at selling homes for top dollar," he continued, "and I want to help these families get the most they can, but trying to sell houses in this condition puts us at a serious disadvantage."

How much of a disadvantage? These neglected, cluttered houses, if they do sell, go for on average $50,000 to $60,000 less than they would have if they were cleared out and cleaned up, he said.

Did you hear that? I don't care if you are leaving all your money to your Jack Russell terrier, $50,000 to $60,000 is real change. Whether you leave your money to your kids or your college, use it to fund your world cruise or your long-term care, $50,000 is a crime to lose out on because you didn't cut through your clutter.

"In most cases," Weaver said, "these homeowners could get rid of 75 percent of what's in their home, still have a full house, and it would look a lot better."

He doesn't need to convince me.

Besides that, they could move beautifully into a simpler, more streamlined home.

I need to step outside for some air.

This is the scenario you and I are going to avoid. Right? With some proactive foresight, all this can be handled so much better.

Now, regular readers of my weekly newspaper column and previous books have heard my harangue about letting go of stuff, getting rid of clutter, cleaning house, and purging. We've been over the benefits of living in a clutter-free, well-organized, well-edited home. We've talked about the good feeling that comes from being able to park both cars in the two-car garage, or to pull a pillow out of the linen closet without having a stack of towels fall on your head, or to have those friends over for dinner because you're no longer embarrassed by your place. Those goals right there should be motivation enough to catapult you off your keister and send you searching for the extra-strength trash bags.

But now here are two more reasons to sort, sell, and purge:

1. **Money.** If you're a homeowner, you are going to lose out on a lot of money if you don't.

2. **Freedom.** Extra stuff acts like an anchor, weighing you down and keeping you from moving forward to a place that is a better fit.

"It breaks my heart to see families in this situation," Weaver said. "I want to help them do this better than I am."

The answer, of course, is to head all this off at the pass. That's part of rightsizing. Whether you plan to stay in your home or move, rightsizing means living with only those items that you need, use, and love, and that serve your life today and going forward. Thus, rightsizing, regardless of how big your home is, requires diligent (and regular) sorting, purging, selling, tossing, donating, and decluttering. This effort will not only lead to a higher quality of life now but will also make the sale of your home, when that day comes, faster and more lucrative.

Far too often, having too much stuff is what stands between many older adults and a simpler, more enjoyable, less stressful, more gracious rightsized life.

Once these people (maybe you) let go, they can clear the biggest and sometimes the only barrier on their path toward a beautifully rightsized life.

"We Are Living Our Best Life"

"The decluttering conversation is always a hard job," said Don Maycott, a Realtor with eXp Realty and cofounder of the eXp Seniors Network representing The Villages in Central Florida. That's a good niche: The Villages is the largest retirement community in the world, with 80,000 homes inside 80 square miles. Maycott lives there with his wife, Jeannine.

"You don't want to offend or upset the homeowner," he said, "but you also want to help them sell the home quickly for the best price. So you're walking on eggshells."

I know the type. How do you tell Mrs. McGillicuddy, who is seventy-five, that it's time to let go of her son's Cub Scout uniform, which she has in a box with the dead corsage she wore to senior prom, which she went to with a guy she didn't marry?

"Real estate agents have to be sociologists, psychologists, archeologists, and diplomats," Maycott said.

He leads by example. In 2015, when Don and Jeannine Maycott were both fifty-five, they moved from their 3,600-square-foot, single-family home in Atlanta to a 1,600-square-foot single-family home in The Villages. "We asked our two grown children if they wanted anything," he said. Each took a few things. Then he and his wife tagged what was going to Florida and put the rest in a garage sale. What was left went to charity. "It worked very well for us. We are living our best life."

Now he freely tells his story to others. "It's the right move for so many people, and too few make it," he said.

I was curious to know, however, how his wife viewed the transition. "The move wasn't *that* simple," Jeannine conceded. "I had to give up a home I had lived in for twenty-one years. While I knew Florida would be great, when it came time to say goodbye, it was emotional. It's easier for men than for women."

That said, she's not sorry she made the move. "It was time," she said. "Our house was great while the kids were growing up. They were in walking distance of good schools, but once they were gone, it seemed ridiculous."

She and her husband agreed that once both their kids were out of college and supporting themselves, they wouldn't need the big house anymore, but he was ready to move before she was. Don found the community in The Villages. Though she was reluctant, he insisted they see it. They visited three times, the first two times they stayed a week, and then the last time for a month, in August. "If you can take Florida in August, that's the real test," Jeannine said.

She discovered she liked both the senior community lifestyle and the weather. "I love all the activities. You can go out every single night and listen to a different band for free. Plus, I wanted a change of weather. I always got depressed during Georgia winters."

Being close to family wasn't a priority for them. Even when they lived thirty minutes away from parents and in-laws, "We didn't see them often," she said. "We are tied to each other and our kids, and not so much to the extended family." Their kids, now in their thirties, visit often. The Maycotts cut their living expenses almost in half and sold one of their two cars, which they no longer needed.

They donated or sold more than half their belongings, she estimates, and brought about 40 percent with them. "Much of what we gave away was too heavy for Florida. I wanted a lighter look." She hasn't missed anything she let go.

However, if she had to do it over, she would make one change. "I would have taken more time to find the right house. We rushed to buy. The house we got is cute, but I would have liked one a little larger."

On the bright side, "I have a lot less to clean and a lot more to do." As for how she feels being in a senior community, she laughs: "We're among the younger ones, and yet I never feel like, ick, everyone is so old. Never. These senior citizens do more than I do. They are not holed up in their houses. They are out enjoying life."

And so is she.

Twelve Ways to Get Out from Under a Full House

Because his good example only gets him so far with potential sellers, Don Maycott, like Jerry Weaver, asked me what advice I could offer for those held hostage by their stuff in their outsized homes. So I cobbled together my best advice to help this group cross the bridge between stuck in the past and a lighter, better future and came up with these twelve tips for all of us:

1. **Don't wait till you sell.** If you clean house now, when you do want to move, that much less will hold you back. Sorting through and getting rid of stuff does not get easier as you age. But if you make that initial cut, and then make streamlined living a lifestyle—that is, you make it a conscious practice to keep only what you need, use, and love, and get rid of the rest—you will be way ahead.

2. **Beware of this word: later.** By not waiting to thin out your closets and cupboards, shelves and drawers, attics and basements, you'll get to enjoy the benefits of living in a cleaner, more streamlined home. You'll gain the peace of mind of knowing that you will not leave a mess for your loved ones and that if you do decide to move, the job will be that much easier and less expensive. Movers charge by weight and time. Your house will show better and thus sell faster for a better price (as you'll see in Chapter 7). And here's another bonus: if you have a big yard sale, you'll get a pile of cash.

3. **Have those conversations.** Ask your children, other family members, and friends what items they want and if they're willing to take them now. Ask your kids or grandkids to help you tackle the attic, the basement, and everything in between. They may groan, but this is your chance to impart the family history. Some of it might even stick.

4. Get help. If your kids aren't available to help, professionals are. Contact the National Association of Productivity & Organizing Professionals to find a trained organizer near you who can help you sort through your things compassionately and impartially and re-home them. If you're moving, the National Association of Senior Move Managers also has experts who can help you separate what to take from what to let go.

5. Declutter. Some homeowners avoid cleaning house because they can't do it alone and are too embarrassed by the mess to ask for help. Don't be too proud to get help. Professional organizers have seen worse and are trained to deal with this. Real estate professionals agree: decluttering is the number one task more homeowners should tackle to help their homes look, feel, and live better and be worth more.

6. Fix what needs fixing. To get a quick, top-dollar sale, you also want to address deferred maintenance. You may know how to live with the tricky toilet, the room that gets no heat, and the spot in the kitchen that leaks when it rains, but plumbing, heating, or roof repairs left undone turn buyers off. Those who don't walk away will expect a steep discount.

7. Deep clean. Some of us get so used to seeing our homes, we don't notice the cobwebs in the light fixtures, the grime in the grout, the fingerprints on the light switches, and the pet smells. Hire a professional to scour the place inside and out to make it sparkle. Again, the goal is to help you get top dollar as you rightsize into a home and a life that is a better fit.

8. Picture all your stuff in the landfill. Imagine what will happen if you don't thin out your stuff and fix up your place, and if, as a result, you don't attract a good buyer. An investor will likely snap up your beloved home for well under market value, put all its contents into a Dumpster, and remodel it for a fast sale at twice what he paid you for it. We're not going to let that happen, right?

9. Be a good neighbor. If more money doesn't motivate you, maybe this will. A low-price home sale impacts the neighborhood's comps and thus devalues all the houses around you. Do you really want to be that neighbor who lowered everyone's property values? Of course not.

10. Live in real time. Living in the past robs you of the present. How can you enjoy the best of your golden years when you can't park your car in the garage because you have a thirty-year-old crib and high chair in there? Stuff holds you back and weighs you down. Nature shows us everywhere that to grow, living things must shed. Think of a tree that must lose all its leaves to experience new growth. Humans should do the same.

11. Focus on the pluses. Not to put too big a bow on this, because shedding is hard, but one reason so many older adults can't let go and move forward is because they are so busy clinging to their past (which is not coming back, sorry) that they can't enjoy the present or embrace what's ahead, or what could be. Picture what your new life could look like. Visualize the upside of rightsizing: not having to care for more house than you need; having less yard to maintain and more discretionary income; enjoying the freedom to travel more; having the convenience of a house better designed for you, like one with a downstairs master; and, not least, knowing the enormous gift you will be giving your heirs. (Believe me.)

12. **Let go in stages.** Purge what you can before you list your house, and then box up what you're not using: extra linens, dishes, clothes, books. That will make cabinets and closets look more spacious and help buyers see the house, not the stuff. Move those boxed items neatly into the (now cleaned out) garage or into a temporary rented moving container, such as PODS. (Not, have mercy, a storage facility.) Once the house sells, revisit these items. After you've experienced what living with less feels like, you may realize you don't need many or any of these items at all. We'll learn more about that in Part Three: What Every House Needs—and What It Doesn't.

Decluttering and downsizing your stuff, regardless of your age or whether you're moving, is a gift to yourself, to your loved ones, to your neighbors, and to your future. And it removes one of the main hurdles that stand between you and a better place.

Matt Paxton Wants You to Tell Your Story

When I called downsizing guru Matt Paxton, I knew that once we got to talking, we may never stop. Such is the territory we both know, love, and share: people, their houses, and their stuff.

The former host of *Hoarders,* which ran for fifteen seasons, and current host of PBS's *Legacy List with Matt Paxton,* Paxton and his team have visited scores of homes across America helping families unpack not only their stuff, but also the stories buried within.

Both Paxton and I unwittingly became downsizing experts out of personal experiences. I wrote my first downsizing book while in a state of PTSD after clearing out my parents' home of fifty years. Paxton lost his dad, stepdad, and two grandfathers in rapid succession, and cleared out each of their homes.

It changes a person.

Curious to get his take, I asked him to comment on the following:

On the Difference Between Hoarders and Downsizers . . .

Hoarding is a mental disorder where people need to acquire a large number of items to feel worthy, Paxton explained. Invariably, these people have suffered a massive trauma and are looking to compensate for that. They are looking for happiness or comfort in stuff. When working with a hoarder, you have to address the trauma behind the behavior and help them remember a time when they felt love in their life.

People who need to downsize often worked really hard to get where they are. They remember having nothing. Their insanely hard work ethic makes it harder for them to let go of what they worked so hard for. When dealing with downsizers, the key is to celebrate their life of hard work, capture their stories, and let the stuff go.

On Motivating Folks
Who Need to Downsize . . .

I ask them to choose the five or six items that mean the most to them and their family and talk about why. Everyone should do this. Your story doesn't need to be perfect. Just record what you know, take a picture, and attach the image to the story. Tell your stories to family members over Zoom and hit record. Once you preserve those five or six items and their stories, it's a lot easier to get rid of the fifteen potholders. Because it's never about the stuff; it's always about the stories. If the person, say it's a grandma, is moving, keep the focus on why she is moving. If it's to be near her kids and grandkids and closer to better health care, that vision gives her purpose.

On Financial Versus
Emotional Worth . . .

If you decide to get rid of an item, your next decision is whether to sell or donate. If you decided to sell an item but don't like the price you're offered, so what? Don't let price stand in the way of getting rid of something you decided you don't want. (Please read that sentence again.) I don't care what any item is worth financially. I want to know how much it's emotionally worth.

On What You Wish
More Americans Knew . . .

One, you already have enough stuff to live. You do not need more stuff. Everything else is a want. Two, my TV show makes the job of downsizing and decluttering look a lot easier than it is. We have a team that comes in and works nonstop.

Realistically, it takes most people trying to downsize about six months if you work at it an hour a day. If you feel overwhelmed, call in a professional to help.

And three, sorry to bring this up, the clock is ticking. Do you want to spend your time dealing with, maintaining, and paying for the overhead to house your stuff, or free yourself to have more time and money to spend on life and its experiences? Getting rid of stuff helps you make room for the life that you want. You should be in the Keys having drinks with your wife, not sorting through your attic.

On What to Say to Retired Empty Nesters Still Living in the Home Where They Raised the Kids . . .

I would ask them why they are living in a storage unit for their adult children. Your house is not a storage unit. Their stuff is their responsibility. Set a firm date for them to get it. If they haven't gotten it by then, it's yours to get rid of.

On Minimalist Rules to Live By . . .

What you bring in should equal what you take out. If you get a new pair of jeans, get rid of a pair. Also, get rid of anything that is part of your fantasy life. Those ice skates, that surfboard. The dress that has not been your size for five years. At the end of the day, minimalism is keeping only what actually serves your life now.

A New Way to Preserve Old Memories

When Heather Nickerson's mother died unexpectedly in 2016 at age sixty-five, she wished she had paid closer attention to her mother's stories. "She had an estate plan, so her financial affairs were in order, thankfully, but her stuff was overwhelming," Nickerson said. "I remember sitting on the floor of her closet in tears because I had no way of knowing what she would want me to keep. I wanted to hold onto what mattered, but I had no way of knowing what did. I figured there must be a better way."

Now there is. In 2021, she and a former colleague partnered up to form Artifcts, an online platform for those who want to preserve the stories behind their stuff for future generations. Part family museum, part storage locker, part scrapbook, Artifcts lets those who love their keepsakes preserve them in a shareable digital collection. The truly motivated can upload audio or video files, too.

Just think of all the times your parents or grandparents told you stories, and you didn't pay attention. This site would fix that. "We end the mess and solve the mystery," said Nickerson. She and fellow cofounder, Ellen Goodwin, are former CIA agents. (Who better?) "Ellen and I worked as intelligence analysts for the CIA for ten years. Like most CIA types, we are driven and share an insane desire to gather data."

They launched the platform in August 2021, and two years later, nearly 3,000 members had collectively "artifcted" over 10,000 items. Costs range from free to upload five artifacts to $89 annually to upload unlimited items—a lot less than a storage unit.

Examples of items members don't want around the house but still want to remember might include a special piece of kid art, an old letter jacket (better a photo of the jacket with a caption you can easily visit than the actual jacket in a box in the basement), and travel mementos.

"We very often see that once someone has stored an item and

preserved its meaning online, they let it go," Nickerson said. "Others upload pictures and descriptions of items they keep and plan to pass down. Some use the platform to send files to their insurance companies, or to link to their estate plans, trusts, or wills."

Speaking of which, who inherits the account after the person who formed it is gone? Whomever you designate. And that heir can then decide to keep the virtual collection; pass it along to someone else; download the information, export, and store it; or close the account and never visit again.

However, if you've proactively stored your meaningful items online, you've at least lightened the load and opened the door to the possibility that the next generation will know the stories behind the stuff.

CHAPTER 7

Couple Buys Two Homes for the Price of One

Not everyone needs to run the numbers to know whether they should move or not. For Katie and Thad Seymour, the decision was quick and clear.

"I never thought I would want to leave my lake house," Katie Seymour told me when I stopped by the Lake Mary, Florida, home she and her husband, Thad, had lived in for thirty-one years.

Katie had asked me to come by to offer some staging tips to help the house sell. As she showed me around the lovely 3,000-square-foot lakefront pool home, where their three children had grown up, I couldn't help but pry.

"Why?" I asked.

I'm always curious to learn what motivates those long settled in a family home to voluntarily roll up their rugs, empty their closets and drawers, unpack their attics, and move. It takes courage, vision, faith, and fortitude, qualities you don't see often enough. While more retirees—Katie's sixty-five and Thad's sixty-seven—should move once their kids are launched, as we've discussed, many stay tethered like root-bound oaks to homes that no longer serve them.

Not Katie and Thad.

"We knew we would eventually sell the family house and move to something more fitting for empty nesters," Katie told me, adding that Thad embraced the idea first.

Excuse me, can we bottle that attitude and wisdom?

"Though I loved the house," Thad said, "I didn't have the same emotional attachment to it as Katie. I was ready to let go and move on to the next chapter. The amount of work involved in keeping it up felt like more every year."

I could relate. Anyone who has owned a big home knows it can turn into a microeconomy.

Katie hit her tipping point a few months earlier when she learned their first grandbaby was on the way. "The baby changed everything," she said and literally started packing with her eye on Milwaukee, where her daughter, son-in-law, and soon-to-be-born grandbaby live.

Their son lives just an hour and a half away in Chicago, and five of Katie's siblings also live nearby. While a Wisconsin home made sense, they didn't want to abandon Florida and all the connections and friends they had made there. Soon the answer was clear: they would buy two smaller, lower-maintenance homes for the price of the one they were selling.

And that's the plan.

"We'll spend more time with family, less time taking care of our home, and still have people to visit us in Florida to have all the fun that is here," Katie said.

"I used to think all the kids would come to the family house and I would host Easter and all the birthday parties," she added, "and so I would need the big house, but the truth is, they don't come. They have busy lives and can't get the time off, and that will only get more difficult when the grandkids come along. It's easier if we go to them."

After exploring several neighborhoods, they bought a smaller (2,300-square-foot) home in Lake Nona, a planned community about twenty-five miles south of their current home. Katie describes it as "lock and go." The house has almost no yard. The weekly fee to maintain the small strip of grass out front is $15, which sounds great after years of paying several hundred dollars a month on pool and yard maintenance. The home still has four bedrooms, so the kids and ultimately grandkids can visit.

And they'll want to. The property has access to three pools, a ropes course, and hiking and biking trails. It is walking distance to restaurants, just six miles from the airport, and twenty minutes from Orlando's major theme parks.

Next, the Seymours will find a small, single-family home in Wisconsin "after we sell this," Katie said, which reminds me that I am supposed to be helping her stage. I apply the advice I've doled out in my column and followed myself many times: deep clean, declutter, de-pet (that is, remove pet paraphernalia), depersonalize, depoliticize, de-religionize, and sell a lifestyle—iced tea pitchers and glasses on the patio table.

As Katie and Thad explained what lay behind their decision to make their life-changing, rightsizing move, I kept thinking: *These guys are getting it right. They thought through what they want their lifestyle to be in retirement and what matters. They figured out where they want to live, how much house they need and want to maintain, and how they want to spend their time and money. They're living with intention, and I'm impressed.*

They're also proving that rightsizing in your later years doesn't always mean downsizing; it can mean resizing. As we talked, I gathered several pieces of their good advice for others contemplating such a move:

- **Don't wait.** Maintaining a large home doesn't get easier as you get older. Nor does moving. Katie and Thad have seen what happens when people wait too long to move. They told me about a couple they know in their eighties who didn't keep up with their home's necessary maintenance. Now their house needs so much work they will have a hard time selling it for anywhere near what they could if they had maintained it. "We didn't want that to be us," she said.

- **Try before you buy.** Echoing the advice we heard from Liz Hicks in Chapter 5, the Seymours felt that knowing an area well before buying a home there was essential. They spent the last two summers in Milwaukee, so they know what it's like and know they'd like to live there.

- **Get a pre-inspection.** To head off any issues that could surface during a buyer's home inspection, Katie and Thad had their home inspected before they listed it. (Another smart move.) That's when they learned they had to replumb their home because its water pipes were made of polybutylene, a resin material common in homes built in the 1980s and early 1990s. In 1995, builders stopped installing polybutylene pipes because some failed, and insurers stopped insuring homes that had them. "If a buyer can't get insurance, that would be a deal breaker," Thad said. "Better we found out beforehand."

- **Focus on the upside.** Clearing out a home you've lived in for years, let alone decades, and getting it ready to sell is overwhelming. The task is often so daunting many hit the default button and stay put. Not the Seymours: "We're looking forward to spending less time on a home, yard, a pool, and our things and to spending carefree summers in Wisconsin and winters in Florida."

- **Don't listen to the kids.** "The kids wanted us to keep the house," Katie said. "'Don't ever sell it,'" they said. 'We want to bring the grandchildren back.'" Easy for them to say. They don't have to maintain it. Fortunately, parents don't always do what their kids want them to do. Sometimes, they do what's best.

Home Staging Tips for a Fast, Top-Dollar Sale

Just as we discussed the importance of decluttering in the last chapter, another tried-and-true home-selling practice is staging. Katie called me to help her because she knew me when I was a live-in home-stager. Not that I would recommend that vagabond existence, which involved living in other people's homes for sale, decorating them with my furniture, and keeping them show ready. But I do know what works.

If part of your rightsizing journey involves selling the home you're in and if getting top dollar and a fast sale matters, here are six proven ways to set the stage:

1. **Be organized and tidy.** The goal here is to encourage buyers who walk in to think, *Wow, if I lived here, my life would fall into place, too.*

2. **Remove the knickknacks.** Keep only large accessories out, say, those larger than a cantaloupe, and eliminate the small ones.

3. **Give every room a purpose.** I don't mean a purpose as in, this is where the couch goes. Add some life. Set out a Scrabble game or jigsaw puzzle (here we play games) in the family room, set the dining room table for a dinner party, put a lemonade pitcher and glasses out on the patio, hang a party dress in what could be a teenage girls' bedroom, prop a cookbook up in the kitchen, featuring an appealing healthy recipe, like tomato soup. (No meat, nothing too fattening.) You get the idea.

4. **Depersonalize.** Put away family photos; otherwise, buyers will zoom in on your wedding photo when you want them to look at the house. Remove any hint of your religious or political beliefs. (I know, just do it.)

5. **De-pet.** Remove Fido and Fifi and any signs they live there during showings.

6. **Add fresh flowers and greenery.** Make sure all your houseplants look healthy. (Ditch the strugglers.)

Katie and Thad followed the advice (though at one point Katie confessed they wanted to burst into tears at how overwhelming it was), but they made it. "I took three carloads to the donation center, and it felt so good to give things away to people who might need it," she said. "I feel lighter already."

P.S. They got four offers in twenty-four hours, two over the asking price. Staging works.

Now it's your turn to dream. What does your rightsized life look like, and what will it take to get you there?

Upside, Downside, Vision

What's motivating you to rightsize? (Upside)

_____

_____

_____

_____

_____

In a word, how powerful is that desire?

_____

What's holding you back? (Downside)

_____

_____

_____

What would you have to do to clear these hurdles?

_____

_____

_____

What does your rightsized life look like? (Vision)

_____

_____

_____

_____

_____

_____

Part Two

How They Did It

God gave us the gift of life; it is up to us to
give ourselves the gift of living well.
—Voltaire

bet that what most of you reading this book want to know is this: If you go through with a rightsizing move, whether to a new house or a new town, and you drum up the courage to make a move that will bring about a dramatic life change, will you be glad you did? Or will you regret it?

To find out if the grass is really greener, who better to ask than those who've completed their rightsizing journey? In the pages ahead, we'll meet people who had the courage and forethought to make a change and find a home that was a better fit, or who built or remodeled a home to better suit their needs going forward. These rightsizers range in age from their fifties to their nineties.

Let's learn from them as they share their journeys, worries, regrets, discoveries, mistakes, joys, and collected wisdom.

CHAPTER 8

Empty Nesters Build Rightsized Dreamhouse

When their youngest of three children was fifteen years old, Paula and Paul Loftus ran the numbers. After a brief analysis, they foresaw that this child, too, just like his older brother and sister, would very likely finish high school and go away to college.

And that meant one thing: Paula and Paul, who were both in their fifties, would be left with too much house. "Once the last kid was launched, the house would be more than we needed, and certainly more than we wanted to take care of," Paula said.

The Loftuses are the refreshing exception. Most empty nesters default into staying in the family home for one of three reasons, or all of them:

- **Denial.** The kids love this home, moving would break their hearts, and anyway, we're not really getting older.

- **Complacency.** Moving is too much effort. This house is so full of everyone's stuff it would take dynamite and an archeologist to get us out.
- **Fear.** Where would we go? What would we do with the leftover furniture? How would we ever fill out all those change of address forms? What if the kids boomerang back home? *Blah, blah blah.*

Paul and Paula defied gravity and made an exit plan. They knew they wanted to stay in their town of Winter Park, Florida, so they bought a lot within half a mile of their family house with an old structure on it that they would tear down. They spent the next few years envisioning, designing, and building their downsized dreamhouse.

In 2019, when their youngest indeed went off to college, they traded their 6,000-square-foot, six-bedroom home of seventeen years for a 3,200-square-foot, four-bedroom house with a basement. To make the new place work, they sold, donated, or tossed more than half of their household contents and are enjoying the lightness of their new rightsized life.

Shortly after they were settled, my husband and I had the honor of being their first dinner guests. "As long as I can bring my laptop and ask questions," I said, only half-joking, when Paula, a friend for years, invited us. (Woe be to those who befriend a columnist.)

> We had a great house, and we had a lot of fun there. We hosted a lot of school and work functions, but it served its purpose.
>
> —Paula Loftus

After the home tour, I settled in the seating area next to the big open kitchen, popped open my laptop, and popped off some questions. How? Why? And what did you learn?

"We had a great house, and we had a lot of fun there. We hosted a lot of school and work functions, but it served its purpose," said Paula, adding that she's had no problem walking away.

Paul, a business consultant, sees nothing but upside. "We got rid of the payroll that went along with maintaining a large property and all that comes with it," he said, referring to the former lakefront home, which sat on over an acre and had a pool. The new home is on a quarter acre. He estimates their monthly household expenses will be a third of what they were.

Less home, less responsibility, and more cash mean more freedom to enjoy all the plans they have for the next phase of life.

Dream It, Build It, Live It

Such a lifestyle-change stage doesn't just happen. It takes fore-sight, intention, and determination. Here's what Paula and Paul considered as they dreamed, planned, and built their downsized dreamhouse:

- **The architecture.** Because the street they built on had houses dating back to the late 1800s, the Loftuses built an American four-square house, a style popular at the turn of the century. "A modern home would have just been inconsiderate," said Paula. The home features a deep front porch and second-story dormer windows.

- **A chef's kitchen.** "The kitchen is where everyone in our family loves to cook and hang out," Paula said, so they made a big French-inspired kitchen the heart of the home.

- **No dining room.** The Loftuses are known for hosting great dinner parties, but they didn't want a dining room that would often go unused. "Most of the time it's Paul and I and maybe one kid," said Paula. The new home has an eat-in kitchen with a table that can extend to accommodate many guests. (I have since attended two book club gatherings at her home and never for a second missed having a formal dining room.)

- **Multipurpose areas.** Rather than one big room to gather in, the home has several areas for seating or other uses. "A great room backfires," Paula has discovered. "Having more small seating areas means multiple generations don't have to be all fenced in. Older folks can get away from the din of the kids. Others can find discreet areas to work, relax, or talk, but not all in one space."

- **Smaller bedrooms.** While each of their three grown children still has a bedroom in the new house, their rooms are much smaller. "They are coming to visit, not to live," Paula said. When they're not visiting, the rooms are guest rooms.

- **One-level living.** "We wanted a house where we could live entirely on one floor, so we can age here," Paula said. The new home has a downstairs master, and level thresholds even into the shower.

- **Less stuff.** "I gave myself permission to give away all the stuff I had hung onto simply because I had the room," Paula said. (Huge silent cheer!) Did her kids mind that she'd cleared out the stuff they didn't take with them? "Actually, they were thankful that we took that burden away."

- **Great technology.** "Any sentimental longings our

kids had about the move were quickly forgotten when they discovered that we were wired," Paul said, who invested in the latest, up-to-speed technology.

• **And the memories?** "I don't think memories are in a house," Paula said. "They are in the special items you collect that are part of your life." They brought along antique pieces from Paul's mother and the art and rugs they've collected. "Every piece we chose to carry forward means a lot to our family. Getting rid of the rest wasn't hard for me."

Their advice to those too attached to their big house: "Move on. We love our rightsized life. It's liberating."

CHAPTER 9

Hollywood "Fixer" Seeks Downsizing Fix Post Divorce

Before COVID hit, Howard Bragman had two houses and a spouse. Two years later, at age sixty-six, the celebrity crisis manager, known for cleaning up some of Hollywood's biggest messes, was single and living large in half the space he once had. For a sense of what he's dealt with, past clients include Sharon Osbourne, Nick Cannon, Wendy Williams, Chris Brown, and Monica Lewinsky, which just makes me feel grateful I wasn't calling him for representation.

"After I got divorced, I didn't have to downsize. I chose to," Howard told me, when I got to talking about his downsizing process and how he arrived at his gorgeous result. (I had pictures.)

Going into the pandemic, he split his time between a 1,000-square-foot apartment in New York City and a 4,200-square-foot, five-bedroom, five-bath modern farmhouse in Valley Village, a Los Angeles suburb. Once COVID took hold, giving up the apartment made sense since any TV work he did there he would now do remotely.

As for the California house, after he and his husband parted ways, "The place seemed too big," Howard said. "I didn't want the upkeep. I wanted to live differently and to travel more."

He wanted to *rightsize*. He found a two-story, 2,700-square-foot townhome in nearby Toluca Lake. Besides needing a total makeover, it had what he wanted, no more, no less: two bedrooms, a place for an office, room for a gym, a generous great room, a spacious outdoor terrace for entertaining, and access to a pool and Jacuzzi. The bones were good, but the place hadn't been updated since it was built in 1977.

"That was a plus," he said. "I hate paying to rip out someone else's bad renovation. I'd rather pay for no renovation." Although the place didn't have room for his extensive art and photography collection and his combined homes' 5,200-square-feet worth of furniture, that didn't stop him from realizing his vision for his next chapter and a tailor-made life.

Because a true professional knows when to call for help, the Hollywood fixer called on our mutual friend, Beverly Hills interior designer Christopher Grubb, to help the fixer fix his fixer.

Grubb met Howard Bragman in the late 1990s and has worked on several of his homes. "We've been on quite a design journey," Grubb said. "This house is 180 degrees different from his last one, and it perfectly fits who he is today."

Isn't that what rightsizing is about?

Howard bought the townhome in May 2020. He sold his farmhouse that summer and moved into an apartment while he, Grubb, and an architect worked on the remodel. Apart from the structure's clean lines and high ceilings, all that remains of what it once was are a few walls, the stair railing, a built-in bookcase, an office cabinet, which they repainted, and the garage door. They installed new cabinetry, flooring, and fixtures, and used a palette of blues, grays, creams, and taupes to unify the home.

Then they dealt with the excess art and furniture. "What do you love and what will fit?" Grubb said were the defining questions. Using one of my mantras, *choose to keep rather than choose to let go,* Howard started by selecting which big art pieces would stay, and then he and Grubb decorated around them. Among the keepers was an iconic color photo Annie Leibovitz took of the late film director Billy Wilder on Sunset Boulevard. Wilder and Howard were friends.

> MARNI MANTRA:
> Choose to keep rather than choose to let go.

"Art has a funny way of speaking to you and telling you where it belongs," he said. Howard estimates he sold or gifted about thirty-five pieces of "significant" art. Some he sold at auction or through private sales; some went to museums, and several pieces he gave to friends and relatives. After he picked out what he wanted to keep, Grubb created a gallery wall.

"I loved my farmhouse, but this is more my style," Howard said when I asked him if he missed anything from the old life. "It feels great. I feel like I lost weight. I have

> When I visit someone who lives in a much larger, more extravagant home, I appreciate it, but I thank God I don't have it.
>
> —Howard Bragman

everything I need and nothing I don't. When I visit someone who lives in a much larger, more extravagant home, I appreciate it, but I thank God I don't have it. I wish more people knew that if they scaled back, they could be so much happier. I do not regret letting go of anything. They're things."

Let Your Heart Lead the Way

Because going from 5,200 square feet to 2,700 can feel like an amputation, I asked Howard Bragman and Christopher Grubb if they could translate their process into encouraging pointers for others facing similar life and housing transitions:

- **Get out your happiness meter.** "When clients are downsizing, and we are working together to edit what goes and what stays, I start by asking what makes them happiest. Then we look at what fits," Grubb said.

- **Consider your art on loan.** "I look at it this way," Howard said, "I may have paid for the art, but I don't own it. I am only the caretaker so long as I have it. I appreciate that now someone else will enjoy it."

- **Plan to subtract and then add.** Though more than half of Howard's old furniture made the cut, many of the largest pieces did not. "When moving to a smaller space, you actually need to get rid of more furniture than you think," Grubb said, "to make room for some new items you'll need to pull the place together."

- **Enlist a pro.** A professional designer will help you figure out what will work where and what won't. Grubb knew right away that certain pieces wouldn't work, but he let Howard try them anyway. "Christopher would say, 'We'll see,'" Howard said, "when he really meant, 'It won't work.'"

- **Be realistic about value.** "I had a lot of custom furniture made for my prior homes," he said, "pieces that I really loved and paid a lot for but that didn't transfer well to the new home. I learned they were not worth much." He sold some for small amounts and gave a lot away. "New furniture is like a new car, it depreciates the minute you drive it off the lot," Grubb added. Plus, the current used furniture market is flooded.

CHAPTER 10

Aging in Place—Creating a Forever Home

ack in 2014, Bob Thacker, a lifelong marketing executive, had a crazy idea for a house. He just wasn't sure his fiancée would go along. The couple were living in Minnesota, engaged, and facing the question: Whose house will we live in? Yours, mine, or ours?

Like most couples who marry or remarry later in life, Bob and Karen Cherewatuk, a college English professor, had pasts and opinions. When I met them in 2020, he was seventy-two and she was sixty-two, and they had reached an agreement. To understand how they arrived at their novel solution, you need some background.

Karen lost her first husband to cancer. When that happened, she downsized from her former family home to a townhome. After his divorce, Bob also moved from a larger house to a smaller one. "Neither of us really liked each other's homes," he said. Bob also had a Chicago apartment and a North Shore lake house getaway at the time. But none of the homes felt like "theirs," or "what we needed for our future life together."

During this mulling period, Bob attended a tribute for Princeton architect and designer Michael Graves. He and Graves had met twenty years earlier, when Thacker headed marketing for Target and spearheaded the debut of Graves's housewares products in Target stores nationwide. They remained friends.

At the tribute, which featured a retrospective of the esteemed architect's work, Bob noted the Wounded Warrior project homes in Fort Belvoir, Virginia, which Graves designed in 2011 using universal design so injured soldiers could live as independently as possible. Universal design principles involve creating environments so that the widest range of people can use them, regardless of their ability or disability.

Graves could relate. In 2003, a spinal infection left him paralyzed from the chest down and in a wheelchair. He died in March 2015, a year after this tribute.

"When are you going to build homes like this for the rest of us?" Bob asked Graves. Like most aging boomers, Bob could see a need down the road.

"I don't have a client," Graves answered.

"You do now."

There was just one catch . . .

"Karen and I had been looking at houses to buy, but we'd never talked about building one. I wasn't sure she'd sign up for that," Bob said. He had doubts.

When he called his fiancée, she was in India traveling with students and was standing in a cow field. "Don't tell me no until you've heard the whole story," he started as he wound up for his pitch. But before he'd gotten ten words out, she was saying, "Yes! Yes! Yes!"

See, before her husband died, he was in a wheelchair, so she, too, knew the benefits of having a home that could accommodate unforeseen disabilities.

So Graves set to work. Plans for the couple's Forever House were in place in 2014. After Graves died at age eighty, his firm's senior partner, Tom Rowe, saw the project through its completion in late 2016.

And that is how Bob Thacker and Karen Cherewatuk, who married in July 2015, became the first residents of a Michael Graves Forever House, a home for people to live in as they age that doesn't look like a house for the handicapped.

"Nowhere does it have that *eeyew* feel," Bob said. "It's a vibrant, open, healthy, accessible home. We love it, and even more, we love knowing we never have to leave it."

According to the American Association of Retired Persons (AARP), 87 percent of adults over sixty-five want to stay in their homes as they age. Designing and building a home with ageless spaces is a lot easier and cheaper than retrofitting later. However, for those who want to stay in their homes, some thoughtful retrofitting might make it possible.

"It makes so much sense we call it design-*duh*," Bob said. "Accessible homes are good for everyone. What if you need to accommodate a stroller or a visitor with a walker?"

The moves that make the biggest difference are so obvious, for example, why *wouldn't* you make a doorway 36 inches wide instead of the standard 32 inches?

Good point. "Today's homes are built for able-bodied, right-handed young men of average height. That's not most of us," he adds.

"Ours is not a high-end house," Bob said. "It's a middle-class home in a modest neighborhood in the heart of Northfield, Minnesota. We're more *Better Homes & Gardens* than *Architectural Digest.*"

But it's perfect for them now—and twenty years from now. "We both came from loss, but today we have a great life and many blessings," he said; a blended family of four adult children and seven grandchildren are among them.

For his part, however, the biggest blessing is that she said yes—twice.

Ten Ways to Design a Home for the Ages

With nearly nine out of ten seniors saying they want to age in place, designing homes for an aging population should be a priority for all home builders. Here are ten Forever-House inspired ways to design an ageless space:

1. **Remove entry hurdles.** Make transitions from house to outside or garage smooth and at grade level.

2. **Widen doors.** Make doorways wide enough to accommodate a wheelchair. The front door should be at least 42 inches wide, and interior doors 36 inches. Where possible, use sliding or pocket doors instead of swinging ones, or consider no doors where practical.

3. **Consider an open floor plan.** It's easier to move furniture than walls.

4. **Add lever handles.** On doors and faucets, use levers

instead of knobs. Grabbing a doorknob can be difficult for arthritic hands. Consider motion-activated faucets and doors.

5. **Eliminate stairs.** For anyone on wheels, steps are a challenge. Stairs are also often difficult for anyone who has trouble walking. One solution is to choose a single-level home, eliminate transition steps, and put in smooth, hard flooring. Avoid carpet. Moving a primary bedroom downstairs also helps homeowners avoid stairs and stay in their homes. However, as you'll see in the next section, home elevators have become increasingly popular, as have stair lifts that give those who can't climb stairs a ride.

6. **Fortify the bathroom.** Besides making sure the walk-in shower is curbless and wide enough for someone to roll into, the couple installed three-fouths-inch-thick plywood behind the sheetrock-and-tile walls, so grab bars could be installed anywhere, not just where there happened to be a stud. They also installed lower sink counters so someone seated can access them.

7. **Raise plugs.** Standard height for outlets is twelve inches from the floor. Raise them to eighteen inches so someone in a wheelchair or who has difficulty bending can reach them.

8. **Choose drawers over cabinets.** Just as swinging doors are challenging to get around in a wheelchair, so are cabinet doors. Opt for pull-out, under-counter kitchen drawers instead of cupboards.

9. **Make it moveable.** Rather than a permanent kitchen island, consider one that moves like a piece of furniture, and that raises and lowers.

10. **Drop windowsills.** In living areas, the Forever House places windows twelve inches off the floor instead of at waist level so those sitting get a better view of nature.

Fixing to Dwell? Give Home a Lift

If your location is perfect but your house isn't anymore, a retrofit may be the solution.

It was for Ann McGee, who loved her home. If you saw it, you would understand. Every room of the 2,800-square-foot Mediterranean-style house in Winter Park, Florida, reflects her well-traveled life, her many friendships, her rich memories. She loves her oasis-like patio. She loves her neighbors and her community.

What she didn't love were her stairs.

At age seventy-three, the retired college administrator, who's had one knee replaced, found that an upstairs primary bedroom was a bit of a pain—literally. She considered renovating to put a bedroom downstairs, but that was too costly. Moving from her home of fifteen years didn't appeal to her either.

When her niece showed her a magazine ad she'd clipped that featured a modern-looking, shaftless elevator powered by air pressure, Ann was intrigued. "It didn't look like any home elevator I'd ever seen," she said. "It looked like a piece of art."

Plus, the installation did not involve knocking out walls or digging under the floor into the foundation as required for traditional shaft elevators. Shaft elevators send cabins through five-by-five-foot (minimum) spaces within walls, while shaftless elevators sit in the open on finished floors. Their see-through cylinders transport passengers from floor to floor using air pressure or cables. Ann talked to a couple of elevator companies that sold pneumatic vacuum elevators and soon after elevated her own home with one.

"I love the look of it," she said of the tube-shaped elevator tucked in just beside the stairs in her entryway. "I worried that it would ruin the aesthetics of my home, but it's enhanced it."

While she doesn't use it every time she wants to go up-or-down stairs, Ann, an avid traveler, uses it for her luggage.

"Hips, knees, hearts, backs, lungs, in-laws, convenience," Dawn O'Connor, owner of Daytona Elevator, rattles off the reasons customers call her. Her family-owned business has been installing elevators since 1987.

To that list, Rich Eller, owner of HomeLift, a Nashville-based elevator dealer, adds those people who "flat out are not moving and have got to get upstairs." Given the demographics, the demand for home elevators is quickly growing, and the shaftless models are the fastest-growing sector, he said. "We have a population of people who want to age in place and who are realizing that installing an elevator or a stair lift is a lot cheaper than moving. Builders and architects recognize this is a growing market and are designing more homes with elevators in mind."

> I've just greatly extended the number of years I can live in my house.
>
> —Ann McGee

Although the best time to install an elevator is when you're building a home, adding one later may be easier than you think. Before you give up on the idea because you don't see where you could install an elevator, have an expert out.

The least expensive way to get someone who can't climb stairs up them is with a stair lift. This is a seat that travels straight up a flight of stairs. When you decide to move and put the house on the market, since it's not a permanent installation, it can be removed, leaving just a few holes to be patched.

Ann paid $40,000 for her elevator and feels it will add to her home's resale value, when that day comes. "I feel like having an elevator lets you tap into a whole new market," Ann said.

Meanwhile, she said, "I love where I live and how I live. I wanted to buy more time in this house, and I did."

CHAPTER 11

When Rightsizing Means Upsizing

An occupational hazard of being a real estate agent is that while scouting sale properties for a client, you can walk into a home you suddenly have to have. "We were not looking to move," said Suzanne White, a fifty-eight-year-old Realtor from Memphis. "My husband and I had never discussed it."

However, like so many couples, they had had the *wouldn't it be nice if . . .* conversations. She'd always wanted a pool and the space to host big parties. He wanted a music room and a woodshop.

"But these were casual wishes," Suzanne said. Not enough to drive them from their 2,800-square-foot home of seventeen years, where they had raised their blended family of four now-grown children, and from a neighborhood and neighbors they loved.

That all changed in the fall of 2020, when Suzanne walked into the 4,225-square-foot home in Cordova, Tennessee, a fifteen-minute drive from their East Memphis home. "I quickly saw that it checked all the boxes," she said.

Uh-oh.

The storybook brick house with its gabled roof sat on a one-acre lot and had a pool, a detached garage perfect for a woodshop, a covered porch, all downstairs bedrooms, turnkey finishes, lots of room inside and out for parties, and plenty of yard for their two large sheepadoodles to romp.

She went home and told her husband, "You need to come look at this house. But don't worry, we're not moving."

Uh-huh.

By that afternoon they were writing an offer.

Not everyone moving into a forever home moves into a smaller place. In fact, the downsize surprise is that half of adults over age fifty-eight didn't downsize in their last move. As we mentioned in Chapter 2, most same-sized, and three in ten bought houses over 3,000 square feet, according to the National Association of Realtors' 2023 Home Buyers and Sellers Generational Trends Report.

> Not everyone moving into a forever home moves into a smaller place. In fact, the downsize surprise is that half of adults over age fifty-eight didn't downsize in their last move.

"Some might say, I even used to say, it's stupid to upsize at this stage of life," Suzanne said. "But now when people ask, 'Do you really want that much yard?' We answer, 'Yes!' We are in our pool all the time, and we can always say, 'Party at our place!'" Shortly after they moved in, they hosted a sit-down dinner party for sixty.

Not Settling

Suzanne and Mark White, age sixty, are among a growing number of adults over age fifty-five who are bucking tradition. Typically, when the kids leave home, the parents downsize. However, more couples at this stage of life are choosing to upsize or same-size to a home that offers more of what they want, according to the NAR report.

"The move to get more house in their golden years marks a significant shift away from previous real estate norms," said Andrew Rosen, a certified financial planner and president of Diversified, a Delaware-based wealth-management firm. Other major moving motives, he adds, are family, weather, and money. "No state income tax is a massive influence. People ask, 'Why am I paying taxes for schools here and my kids aren't in school?'"

Those moving in their golden years are not only gravitating toward larger homes but also toward their dreams. "What they are not doing is settling," he said. "In the past, once people retired, they would often stay in their homes, and say, 'This is fine. We'll stay.' Now, more are saying, 'I've always wanted this dream,' and they're going for it. They are upsizing, changing locations, and pursuing that dream to live on a lake, at the beach, or in the mountains, and they are making sure they have room for the kids and grandkids to visit."

Some also want to make sure they have room to bring in live-in help if they need it later.

Suzanne agrees. "In addition to a desire to live larger, what I also see among my retired clients is they are not as willing to settle. Where in the past, they would have sacrificed getting the house they wanted so they could get in the right school district, now they know what they want and are getting it."

Common items on the wish list: neighbors not too close, an upgraded kitchen, a soaker bathtub, a sewing or craft room, enough space in the laundry room for an ironing board, a covered porch, and a big pantry.

This group can often get what they want because, unlike younger buyers, they can afford to be patient. More often they can buy their new home without having to sell their current home first, which takes away pressure and gives them the luxury of taking their time to find what they want.

"When you remove the contingency of needing to sell to buy and of needing to be in a desirable school district, the options grow significantly," Suzanne said, adding that if she and her husband had bought the same house they did in their old East Memphis neighborhood, which was in a better school district, it would have cost twice as much (over $800,000 as opposed to $417,000).

Today, the Whites enjoy every bit of their house, yard, and especially their pool. "We loved our other house, but this one gives us so much more room to have the lifestyle we want." Mark, who works from home, has a dedicated office downstairs, a music and podcast studio upstairs, and his longed-for woodshop in the detached garage. Upstairs, Suzanne also has the perfect enclave for her office. All the bedrooms are downstairs, which she sees as a plus for when they get older.

As for downsides, she said, the utility bills almost doubled, and they lost their neighborhood feel, but, "Two-and-a-half years later, we still drive up and can't believe this is our house. It's like we have our own retreat."

They plan to stay as long as they can afford it and enjoy it, whether that's five, ten, or twenty more years. "I don't know what eighty looks like, but we will stay for however long this is the life that makes us happy."

Oops, Our House Is Too Small

My husband and I are also among those who upsized to rightsize. When DC and I got married in 2016, we were in our fifties. I had just published *Downsizing the Family Home*. I still had PTSD from cleaning out my parents' house and from moving and staging six houses in four years. The memories of the big house in Colorado, and how it had weighed me down and become a millstone, were also still fresh.

In short, I was *over* the big house.

As we looked for houses, that big-house fatigue combined with the fact that DC and I were empty nesters all influenced what we—at least I—was looking for. His three adult children were working professionals; two were married and starting families. My two were attending college out of state. Two guest rooms should have been enough. So when we found the Happy Yellow House, a 2,600-square-foot Mediterranean two-story in a community I loved, within walking distance to shops and restaurants, and a small, no-maintenance courtyard out back with a fountain, it felt like relief. I was sold.

Two years later, I wasn't so sure. Yes, I welcomed the simpler lifestyle. However, our home simply couldn't accommodate our blended family. The kids were sprinkled across four states. When they visited, they needed a place to stay. As they were coupling up and having children, five grew to ten. If I wanted to have the family home, and I did, if I wanted to be the matriarch at the center of this crazy patchwork family, and I did, and if I was ever going to create unity among these adult children who didn't grow up together, which I did, it wouldn't happen in this house. Plus, we now had two dogs, and that charming courtyard felt a little cramped.

We undershot it.

I dreaded sharing these thoughts with DC. After all, I had picked the house I wanted. I remember the evening clearly. I took a deep breath and said, "Honey, I think we need a bigger house." There. I said it. I braced myself for a negative reaction.

Instead, to my surprise, he smiled and said, "I was just waiting for you to realize that."

He'd known all along.

Six months later, we moved around the block just nineteen doors down to the Happier Yellow House, which was 1,000 square feet larger. The home had a downstairs primary bedroom, a separate office (before, my desk was in the great room along with the television and kitchen table), three full guest rooms upstairs with two bathrooms, an upstairs landing area with a pullout sofa, and a balcony terrace with a small kitchen. The house also had a large yard for the dogs.

Now when the kids come with their significant others and children in tow, they have plenty of room upstairs and away from us.

And you know what? It's just right.

Like Jo Stewart said in Chapter 5, we had to get it wrong to get it right.

CHAPTER 12

His and Hers Housing—When Couples Don't Agree

Like many couples, Diane and Norm Bergan, who were eighty-four and eighty-one, respectively, when I spoke with them in spring of 2023, disagreed on the best housing situation for their senior years. Diane wanted to move out of their two-story, 3,600-square-foot home in Flower Mound, Texas, near Dallas, to a smaller house with less upkeep. She gravitated toward living in a community of friends her age, with socials, dances, and other activities. Norm, who likes to tinker in his garage and do home-maintenance projects, wanted to stay put.

They were at an impasse.

When they noticed that a new retirement community was going up about an hour's drive from their home, they made a deposit to reserve a two-bedroom, two-and-a-half bath apartment on the top floor of a five-story building. The apartment would overlook a pond and give way to a view of city lights at night.

"We weren't thinking we were actually going to move in," Diane said. "We thought, 'You never know when you get into your eighties how you're going to feel in a year, or in a week.' We thought of it as an insurance policy."

When the apartment was ready, Diane had warmed to the idea of living in a simpler, smaller place where so much was taken care of for you. "I'd gotten to the point where the house was too much to keep up."

But Norm hadn't.

The Bergans' main home sits on 1.3 acres and has a large workshop, where Norm spends much of his time. "Norm fixes what he can around the house," she said, "but the property needs a lot of work."

"I love doing projects around the house and in my workshop," he said. "Take that away from me, and that's my identity. Sure, the senior community has all kinds of exercise programs and swimming pools, but that doesn't pique my interest."

They went back and forth discussing where they should live and which arrangement best suited them and arrived at an unconventional solution: Norm would stay at the main house. Diane would move into the 1,320-square-foot apartment. "This way we got to test the waters," Norm said. "If the arrangement wasn't working, we could make a U-turn. Our options were open."

Keeping the big house while testing out the new apartment gave them the security of knowing they could always sell the new place and stay in the house if that's what they wanted. For them, keeping their options open was comforting.

"The whole premise of this place was that if something happened to one of us, we would have a plan," Norm said. While Diane lives independently, other levels of care—assisted living, memory care, skilled nursing—are available should she need them.

When I checked in with them six months into the arrangement, the situation was working.

Diane hasn't looked back. "I love it." she said. "I have not cooked a meal or cleaned my apartment since I moved in." Everything she needs is there: a pool, gym, maintenance people, a variety of classes, security, pharmacy, a nurse, and a secure, gated community.

"I wake up every morning, look out at the view over the pond, and I feel like I'm on vacation."

Meanwhile, Norm works on projects around the house. "It's the best of both worlds," he said. "I don't feel like I have to move prematurely. I am very active. I am not ready to jump into senior living. I'm not sure whether I will ever be."

> It's the best of both worlds. I don't feel like I have to move prematurely. I am not ready to jump into senior living. I'm not sure whether I will ever be.
>
> —Norm Bergan

Keeping the main house added another advantage. Diane didn't feel pressured to take more household items than she needed to the apartment. She brought only minimal furnishings. "I love how simple, clean, and spare everything is." Now that she's learned to live with less, she will have no problem clearing out their house's furnishings when the time comes. "We will have to do what most people do: ask the kids what they want, and sell the rest or give it away."

But how do they feel about living apart? Norm makes the one-hour drive to the apartment twice a week, every Wednesday and

Sunday. Diane has only been back to the house once since she moved in since she's no longer comfortable driving on expressways.

"I'm happy here," she said, "though I'm happier when he visits. Sometimes it's hard to see him leave, but I know he'll be back in a couple days. Meanwhile, I go to all the entertainment, ice cream socials, lectures, and meetings. I've made a lot of friends here."

"Amazingly enough it's going pretty well," he said. "I act like I'm her boyfriend when I come to visit. She's okay with it. She gets the lifestyle she wants, and I get the lifestyle I want. All things considered, it's not bad. When I see her happy, I'm happy. At this moment, I have no question we've made the right choice."

"We have a long-term plan and are easing into it," Diane said. "Some people think it's crazy. Some think it's brilliant. All I know is I am a happy camper."

CHAPTER 13

And Then She's Gone— When a House for Two Becomes Home to One

H*ow do I make this home mine without losing her?* The heart-rending question came in an e-mail from Bob Glockler, age eighty-three, of Leesburg, Florida. Bob had recently lost his wife of fifty-six years.

Now, I have written books about clearing out the family home, about downsizing when you find a mate and blend two homes into one, about what to do with all you own so you don't leave a mess when you die, and now this book on getting just the right house for your golden years, but this topic was a curveball: What should a bereaved spouse do with their late mate's things?

Ugh.

Of course, part of rightsizing means tailoring a home for those who live there. When a home for two becomes a home for one, that one must adapt.

Mr. Glockler wrote:

We (now I) have a spacious 1,600-square-foot, two-bedroom home. What do I do with all her things and pictures? Obviously, I will not, do not want to, forget her, but my lifestyle now changes. How do I shift her clothes out of the big closet and move in mine? Do I give up the king-size bed to make more room in the bedroom? (I do not know for what.) At this point, I am not thinking long term—she died only a month ago. But what if I do finally find a new companion?

Phew. That's a lot to unpack. I needed to sit down, stick my nose in a can of strong ground coffee, and take deep head-clearing breaths.

"I thought you might be interested in my dilemma," he added. "But maybe I am too old for your demographic."

I've got news for y'all: while advanced age is a risk factor for death, none of us is immune, as the pandemic reminded us. What a remaining partner should do with a shared home when death do us part happens is a challenge many of us will face.

My husband lost his first wife to cancer. She died at age fifty-five, suddenly and prematurely. When I met DC the following year, his house clearly hadn't changed much since she lived there.

I had a soft spot for Mr. Glockler. I called him. "I'm not sure I have the answers," I told him. "But I will listen and try." On the phone, he sounded like his e-mail: kind, sensitive, honest, and realistic.

Bob and Mary met in Cape Canaveral, Florida, in 1964, when he was a US Navy officer. He went to open an account at the bank where she worked. He wore his officer whites, and that was it for her. They married the following year.

They settled in New Jersey, where he worked in pharmaceutical management. They never had children. They retired in Leesburg, Florida. Two-and-a-half years earlier, they had downsized from a 2,800-square-foot, lakefront house to the apartment across the lake, which was in a senior community that offered housekeeping and nightly dinners.

"The decision to downsize was simple. It was time," he said.

Mary died peacefully at home, holding his hand. She was eighty-four.

Now what?

We tackled the questions regarding his home one at a time, starting at the front door:

- **The entryway.** "When I walk up, I would like to feel this is my home, and not see a reminder of her. Yet I feel conflicted. I want to make this mine. Is that okay? Or is that the same as saying, 'I don't want her'?" What's there now? I asked. A small table with a doily and a ceramic statue of a troubadour, he said. "Now I would not put a troubadour on a lace doily at the door, but I don't know what I would replace them with either. It's not really me. It's her."

- **Suggestion.** It's not disrespectful to change décor that doesn't reflect you. Just go slow. Remove everything and see how you feel. Live with nothing there for a while. Then consider your own style, what you want to fill the absence. Perhaps a potted palm.

- **The china cabinet.** "Everything in the china hutch is from her family and is nothing I would pick. What do I do with it?"

- **Suggestion.** Thin it out. Display items that do reflect you but leave some empty space. You mention that someday you might have a new companion. If you do, when she comes into your home, she will be asking herself, consciously or unconsciously, *Is there room for me in this person's life?*

- **Her closet.** "Our bedroom has a large walk-in closet, which she used. I'm thinking all her clothes need to go to a thrift shop. When her closet is empty, I will move my clothes in, so they're more accessible. That makes sense, but I'm not sure it's right."

- **Suggestion.** Clothes are among the most difficult items to let go of as they trigger many memories and emotions. For now, consider using her walk-in closet as a way station for all the items you're transitioning out of the rest of the home: the troubadour, items from the china cabinet, her bathroom chair. Park those belongings in the closet and see how you and your house feel with the change. When you're ready, have a friend help you box them up to donate. Then, by all means, move your clothes in.

- **The dresser.** "In our bedroom, she had a five-foot-long dresser with an array of pictures on it, including a few of me. It was a very personal collection to Mary. Do I leave them?"

- **Suggestion.** You answered your question. "*It was a very personal collection to Mary.*" Put the photos away, including those of you. Keep out the ones important to you. Then consider selling the dresser and replacing it with an item you will use.

- **The bed.** "We have a king-size, Sleep Number bed, the kind you can adjust, so it's different on two sides. I do not want to sleep on her side, where she died, so I am only using half a bed. Do I give up the bed?"

- **Suggestion.** Easy. You do not need that reminder. Get a new bed.

As we wrapped up our call, Mr. Glockler said, "You raised a good question. What is my style? My style has been shaped by our life together. Before that, I was a kid, then an officer. I didn't have a style. Who am I separate from her?"

"I don't know either, Mr. Glockler, but I have a hunch you're about to find out."

"I suppose eventually I will look for some companionship," he told me. "Whether we're just friends, or move in together, or wind up getting married, who knows? Although I haven't given it much thought, and it's not something on the calendar, it's not unlikely."

Such is the push-pull of loss and the struggle to find the way, any way, forward.

Now I know this is a tough topic, but hang with me because this is a fact: if you are coupled up and bonded till death do you part, you have a fifty-fifty chance that this will happen to you, and you're going to want these pointers. I don't care how young and healthy you think you are.

Besides working to transition a home from "ours" to "mine," so the house doesn't feel like a shrine, a lot more needs to be done. In response to Mr. Glockner's good questions, I consulted a professional organizer and senior move manager for more tips on how bereaved partners can sensitively and practically disperse their late mate's belongings.

Eight Guidelines When Transitioning Through Loss

Nancy Patsios, of Boston, owns Sort It Out. She often works with clients to help them downsize after they've lost a partner.

When I spoke to Patsios, she was sixty-one and had lost her husband to cancer eighteen months earlier. She brings a first-hand perspective when working with clients to sort through a lifetime of memories.

"It always startles me how different the process is for everyone," she said. As we chatted, we came up with these guidelines for those who've loved and lost:

1. **Don't try to meet anyone's expectations for grief.** It has no timetable. The pace and manner in which individuals grieve is varied and personal. Only surviving partners know when they are ready to make changes in the home, Patsios said. "Some feel paralyzed, while others need to do tangible tasks to help them cope." Don't push the process, but try not to wallow, either.

2. **Expect foggy thinking.** "The brain fog is real," Patsios said. "I could have stared out the window for hours without a thought in my head." Don't make any big decisions, including whether to move, too quickly.

3. **Start with the easy stuff.** When you're ready, begin by getting rid of items you don't need, love, or use that slant toward the partner. For Patsios, that was easy. Her husband worked in property management and often brought home gently used furniture. "We did not share that enthusiasm," she said. "It was easy for me to get rid of what I didn't want in the first place." He also had lots of tools. "I don't need seven hammers. I kept one." Save highly personal items, like clothes and jewelry, for last.

> Homes should reflect the lives of those who live there. They don't need to reflect those who once lived there.

4. **View your décor through a new lens.** I have often said that homes should reflect the lives of those who live there. They don't need to reflect those who once lived there. While the desire to honor a lost loved one is normal, clinging to all their belongings is not the best way to do that. In Mr. Glockler's case, I suggested he try to make his home more gender neutral by removing the feminine touches, like the crocheted doilies and floral pillows his wife had sprinkled around the house.

5. **Consider your visitors.** How do you want guests to feel when they come over? A home that is a shrine to your late mate will telegraph your sadness and make guests feel sad, too. A home that has been appropriately edited and tailored to your life now will put guests at ease by telegraphing that you are adjusting.

6. **Capture the essence.** Rather than leave your late loved one's material presence all over the house, try to capture that person's spirit through a few small objects. For instance, if your partner was a gardener, baker, knitter, or fisher, gather items that reflect those passions: a favorite trowel, a rolling pin, knitting needles, or fishing flies. Then create a discreet vignette that represents the person, and let the rest go. For example, Patsios's dad was a master tailor, and her mom was a seamstress. "I kept their thimbles," she said. She keeps them in her nightstand drawer beside her bed, "so they're close."

7. **Donate with purpose.** The biggest impasse professional organizers run into is clients who say they don't know what to do with the stuff they should let go of.

"Part of that is emotional, but part is practical," Patsios said. They don't want to just throw something useful away. So she works to make sure items go to a cause clients feel good about: a church, a program for at-risk kids, an animal rescue. "When they know the items are being donated meaningfully, it softens the blow," she said. When he's ready, Mr. Glockler will donate his wife's belongings to the hospice and hospital thrift stores she supported.

8. **Make choices now, while you're in control of your decisions.** Leaving clear instructions about what you want done with your belongings later will spare your partner or children the headache and let you "move forward gracefully," Patsios said. "So after you're gone, they don't just pull a big Dumpster onto your driveway." Of his wife's death, Mr. Glockler said, "It happened fast. We had no time to talk about what to do with this or that. I wish we had had more time." We all do.

CHAPTER 14

In Defense of Stuff: "My Objects Are a Museum of a Life Well Lived"

I never meant to hurt anybody, especially not a sweet old woman. But it happened.

Her first e-mail arrived telling me, gently but clearly, that I had made her feel bad or, more specifically, guilty for her desire to keep the things she loved around her.

"Maybe it was the title that enticed me, at my very advanced age of ninety, to actually read a home-decorating column," wrote the reader of my column, who asked me not to use her name.

The column she'd read was about how to put the "you" in your home, but not too much of you; rather, a well-edited representation of you, a decluttered, streamlined you.

When in paragraph three I referred to "those homes," she felt called out. "You said," her e-mail continued, "'those homes' with a slight sneer. I guess you might say that I am living in a similar home."

The offending paragraph went like this:

I'm picturing those homes where the sentimental owners smother every doily-covered surface with memorabilia . . . and where oodles of family photos spread across tables like the tattoo plague. Sometimes, less of "you" is better.

Oh, boy. I am knee-deep now.

Though I am no hoarder, and my home, which I have been in for fifty-two years, is clean, I am surrounded by stories, The objects have behind them stories, wonderful stories. The objects remind me of living memories. I live in what some might call a museum—a museum of a life well-lived.

By now, I have slinked like a skink between the cushions of my chair.

I know you did not mean to do it, but you made me feel guilty for not being more philosophical and for being downright unmotivated to spend the years I have left getting rid of stuff.

What kind of a brute would tell an old woman she has to give up her beloved belongings?

She granted that although she thought it lovely that I could adorn my office with a few personal items that I liked and warmed to, that captured the essence of a memory or two, that was not how she wanted her home.

Some people want a sparse office, others want theirs like mine: filled with books, bulletin boards, a rack for greeting cards, many photos of my kids, and rocks my father and I collected. Oh deary dear, guilt has set in again! My point is everyone does not want to live the same way.

I can now hear the crowd shouting, "Off with her head!"

I do not think you are wrong about getting rid of stuff.

Later, in what became an increasingly endearing e-mail thread, ten exchanges in all, between a humbled columnist and a sensitive, older woman, she wrote: *I am sure you have criteria that I could use to get rid of things.*

I do, I tell her, and ask if I could send her a signed copy of my downsizing book and workbook as a gift. She would like that.

And then came the pivot. The next day, she wrote:

After our discussion, I thought maybe I could really get rid of some things. I know I would be doing my family a favor if I chucked out stuff, and I feel a bit selfish keeping it . . .

I am heartened that she is slowly starting to see my point, harsh and insensitive though I may be.

So I either have to spend time getting rid of things or live with the guilt.

I wisely say nothing.

. . . I know that my progeny will have no trouble throwing out and selling objects, and their houses will have less of me, and I certainly hope more of them, and I suppose that is the way of the world.

Yes.

Maybe one day you could write about an old gal with too many objects writing you a funny note that says it is important for us not to all live in identical houses.

Good idea.

You seem to have a good sense of humor, my new friend wrote in her last e-mail. *I would love to have tea in your neat house and to have you in my museum.*

I would love that, too.

Readers Identify with Elderly Woman's Reluctance to Downsize

After that column ran, I received a torrent of replies from readers. So while I wore the hair shirt, I ran a follow-up column. I acknowledged that, in regard to the ninety-year-old reader who graciously chewed me out for making her feel guilty about clinging to her beloved belongings, I had done some soul searching and asked, Who was I to take that away and deprive her of enjoying them in the years she had left? She put me in my place, out in the thistle patch. Then I let readers have their say:

Marni, I am glad you were called out by that ninety-year-old lady, because I also was rather insulted by your "less of you" column. You hit a nerve. Very few things are more personal than how you run your home. My home has always had lots of photos and original art displayed. They bring joy to me. Like your new friend, my house is neat and tidy. And while some visitors have commented on the "busy walls," most seem to like it. But I don't decorate for them. My home is mine and I don't really care what a professional decorator may think of it.

But, be assured, since I have helped clear out five houses, my own home is constantly undergoing "stuffage reassessment." I do not want to saddle anyone with any more of my treasures than necessary. I turn this into a game. I pretend a new visitor is coming and walk through my house looking at it through these fresh eyes to see what needs to go. Or I play just-one-item, where I walk into a room and get rid of one thing—a book, a DVD, the other day it was a stack of baskets.

These items go into the big go-away box in the garage, where they get a second chance. If I don't fetch them out after two or three months, they go for good.

Patty

Fremont, California

Dear Patty, Thanks for sharing a kinder, gentler way to purge. Downsizing is like dieting. You have to find what works for you.

Marni, I loved your column responding to your ninety-year-old reader. I am an eighty-year-old reader and I, too, love my things. As I dust, memories pour back: Who gave me this as a wedding present fifty-nine years ago? Which son saved his pennies to buy me this little lamb? Oh, here's the clown my husband got me to bring a smile to my face in a down time.

But, and this is a big but, I have started to clean out the attic. Those are the things one can part with. After all, they have been out of sight for years, so how could you miss them?

To do this, you need the right mental attitude. The minute the thought that you'd better get rid of the deadwood crosses your mind, get up and do it! You also absolutely must find someone to help who is not emotionally attached to your things, who can be ruthless and discard without commentary about the who, what, where, when, and why you have them.

Anne

Tavares, Florida

Dear Anne, Congratulations on getting started. Now, when you start cleaning out the downstairs, don't put the stuff in the attic!

Marni, This letter gives us a glimpse into the hearts of our elders. I hope, when the day comes, it will help us deal with their nests with compassion rather than resentment. My mother once commented that, based on her observations of older friends, if you don't clean out your stuff by the time you turn seventy, you are not likely to get it done. I'd better get going!

Connie

Lakewood, Colorado

Dear Connie, We all should!

Marni, I loved the discourse with the ninety-year-old lady who lives surrounded by her memories. I am seventy-eight and my husband is eighty. We love the things around us, but a few years back we began asking our children and grandchildren to not give us anything we had to dust.

It has worked! For Christmas and birthdays, we receive movie passes and gift cards to our favorite restaurants. The only thing we have asked for and not received is more help around the house. I doubt there are any older parents out there who wouldn't appreciate that. Our endurance has decreased, and we don't bend as well anymore. We can get down, but it's a struggle to get up.

Jean

Casselberry, Florida

Dear Adult Children Everywhere, Are You Listening?

Part 3

What Every House Needs—*and What It Doesn't*

Living well and beautifully and justly are all one thing.
—Socrates

Where? In what? With what? Those are the three components of rightsizing. While selecting where in the world you want to live and finding or designing the dwelling that best fits your lifestyle and budget are critical factors, as important is knowing what belongs in your new, beautiful, intentionally chosen, rightsized home. The process involves sorting and eliminating what no longer serves you and what is no longer relevant. However, it also involves keeping and acquiring only material items that elevate you and that support your streamlined, upgraded, rightsized life so you are enveloped in curated quality and not clutter.

To discover that, you have to know how to discern quality in household goods. You need to be able to look past the marketing hype and know the properties to look for beyond the brand. You need to become a student of detail and know how to separate the fine from the mediocre. Only then can you let go of items that don't deliver and confidently acquire items that do.

The following chapters will provide guiding lights, fresh ways to look at your household goods so you can make clear, informed decisions about exactly what to keep, what to let go of, and what to buy better as you outfit your rightsized life. While the aim is to teach you the properties to look for when choosing certain housewares, in doing so I occasionally mention brands that are a good example of the category. This is not because they are the only product in the category that meets the standards. They are not. It's for guidance and reference only.

Now, get ready to embrace the luxury of less.

CHAPTER 15

Buy It Once, Buy It Right

Some people think luxury is the opposite of poverty.
It is not. It is the opposite of vulgarity.
—Coco Chanel

magine opening your home's cupboards and closets, drawers and doors, and finding only wonderful, well-made items that you love, need, and use. And nothing else. You find only household goods that work, last, excel at their jobs, and elevate your quality of life. You have no sheets that don't fit right or breathe, no towels that aren't thirsty, no pans that scorch your food, no pillows that fall flat, no sofas that you avoid because they aren't comfortable. Instead, everything you have is a pleasure to use and look at and live with. It was all money well spent.

Who wouldn't want that?

Unfortunately, many homes are filled with the opposite. They are overflowing with subpar products that aren't quite right, that don't quite work, so consumers buy them wrong again. And again. And homes fill with unsatisfying stuff. This happens because consumers don't always know what makes a basic household product great. They don't know what properties to look for and can't always see beyond the advertising hype and fancy packaging. Or they succumb to a sale, thinking they're getting a bargain, which they later regret.

As a result, many homes today are stuffed with household goods we don't like that much and that don't work that well. Because we feel guilty getting rid of these barely used items, they clog our cupboards, closets, and lives. This problem worsens over time.

Entire industries have formed across North America to help residents pare down and better manage their belongings. The field of professional organizers is exploding. America's 53,000 storage facilities are at 90 percent capacity, with more being built. Sales of storage containers and bins continue to grow. All these efforts serve one purpose—the growing need for consumers to control, corral, and manage their overwhelming and underperforming stuff. Why would anything you love, need, and use be in a storage facility? If you can live without it, then, live without it!

The truth is, no professional organizer, no off-site storage unit, and no number of storage bins will fix the fact that our homes are overfilled with mediocre possessions because we don't buy basic household items right the first time. Thus, our homes clog up with stuff that doesn't lift us up, that doesn't raise our quality of life, and that instead clutters our cupboards, hogs space, and drags us down.

But what if we could take the guesswork out of what works and what doesn't? If we knew how to buy (or rebuy) products that really performed well and delivered, we could avoid filling our homes with subpar possessions that erode rather than enhance our quality of life.

Whether you're choosing cookware, knives, wineglasses, upholstered furniture, sheets, towels, or area rugs, outfitting your homes with only those household products that elevate your life starts with having a fundamental understanding of what to look for.

In the chapters ahead, we will delve into the finer points of living, such as the functional differences between cotton and linen, stainless steel and cast iron, hand-knotted and machine-made, triple and single-milled, and more, all to help you outfit your rightsized home right the first time.

Ultimately, owning fewer, better items leads to living large while spending less, and is the key to gracious, clutter-free, rightsized living. Here's another Marni mantra: *Every day is all there is, so use the good stuff.*

> MARNI MANTRA:
> Every day is all there is, so use the good stuff.

To get there, however, you need to know how to pick out great household products from among a noisy and confusing lineup. We're going to go room by room and figuratively purchase the mainstays of each part of the home.

With a fundamental understanding of the properties that make basic household items deliver and do their jobs superbly, by knowing what works better and why, you will become a more discriminating consumer. As a more educated consumer, you will be able to see through the marketing ploys and buy only those household goods that perform elegantly. Along the way, you can confidently purge cupboards and closets so they can breathe. You will see, your orderly homes will run seamlessly with far fewer friction points.

Just ahead, you will learn dozens of insider trade secrets, as well as what makes some everyday objects we use and abuse get better with age, while others deteriorate and disappoint.

You'll learn why some sheets breathe and age well while others smother us and pill. Why some towels are thirsty and others, though plush, don't dry. Why area rugs have such crazy variations in price, and how to know what really makes a rug valuable. How our choice of pan can make us better cooks.

This information will lift the quality of your daily life as you become a more discerning, confident shopper. After reading it, the hopeful phrase "I'll see if this works," will become "I know this will work."

And here's why I know.

My twenty-year journey as a home design and lifestyle columnist started with my desire to uncover the secrets to living well. For two decades, I have sought answers to hundreds of household questions by interviewing the best experts in every field I tackled. I wanted to learn and then share what I learned, tried, and tested with readers to help them, too, live better, more beautifully, more effortlessly, more elegantly, and more affordably.

When I made a wrong move, I wanted to find out what I got wrong. Frustrated by wasting my money on products that over-promised and underdelivered, I made it my goal to know how to buy everyday household items right. A well-appointed home is one that has just what it needs and no more. And it remains the simple secret to living well.

This is the culmination of that desire.

Own Less, Live More

I don't know about you, but I've had enough. Enough buying and spending, getting and giving, and, well, consuming in general, which is why I was so receptive to the message from born-again minimalist Joshua Becker.

"Own less, live more" is his motto, and, I gently suggest, should be ours. The author of several books and a popular blog on minimalism and host of an online decluttering course, Becker's advice feels like a juice cleanse.

While researching this book, I called him for some ways to both minimize and thus maximize my life. Becker, who's in his late forties, started by telling me about his tipping point back in 2009. He was living in Vermont, working as a youth pastor, married with two young children. Over Memorial Day weekend, he and his wife decided to spring clean. He took on the garage.

The project—moving everything out, sorting, tossing, reorganizing, cleaning, and moving much back in—took the whole day. During that time, he struck up a conversation with his neighbor.

"I was complaining to her about how much time this was taking, and she said, 'That's why my daughter is a minimalist. She keeps telling me I don't need to own all this stuff,'" he said. "I had never heard the term 'minimalist' before."

The concept struck him like a giant storage locker landing on his head.

In that instant, he looked back toward his house. On one side he saw his five-year-old son joyfully swinging on the swing set, and on the other he saw all his stuff waiting to go back in the garage. The disconnect was glaring.

"I realized that not only were my things not making me happy but also that they were taking me away from what did," he said. "My things were taking up my time, money, and focus and taking me away from what mattered to me: my faith, family, and friends."

He went inside and said to his wife, "How about if we purposefully own less?" Having just spent her entire holiday cleaning out the kitchen, she hopped on board.

Over the next few years, they purged about half their belongings, and moved from Vermont to Arizona. Their downsizing allowed them to buy a smaller house (from 2,200 square feet to 1,700) in a nicer neighborhood. As they transitioned toward leaner, cleaner living, he wrote about it.

"Our culture is good at stirring up discontent in our lives," he tells me as our inspiring conversation winds up. "We see advertisements all day long that tell us our life isn't as good as it could be if we bought or ate whatever companies are selling. We are constantly told we need to be consuming more in order to be happier and, without realizing it, we start to believe it."

Rather than buy into society's buy-more mentality, do the opposite, he said: resist. As you thin out your life, your wallet will get fatter, and you will be richer in many other ways as well.

Six Ways to Live Better with Less

While I have long written about the merits of downsizing, Joshua Becker takes that one step further preaching intentional minimalism. Here are some ways he suggests we can all live better with less.

1. **Create a minimalist mindset.** Ask what your life could be like if you weren't weighed down with so much stuff. Consider this thought: "I desire to own less so I can save more money, feel calmer and more peaceful, travel more, and spend less time maintaining and housing my possessions." Having that goal is what helps people follow through, he said. Also keep in mind this life-changing principle: We don't buy things with money. We buy them with hours from our life.

2. Start in an easy place. What's tough to sort out differs for everyone. For some it's their books, sports equipment, tools, hobby stuff, or letters. Don't start there. Begin in a place where you can easily finish and enjoy the results, like the bathroom, living room, or bedroom. "I want people to start in a space where they can sit at the end of the day and feel the difference," he said. As the momentum builds, and it will, move on to the more loaded spaces.

3. Lead by example. If your spouse isn't on board with your minimalist ideas, show the way. Work on your own closet, tools, and hobby supplies.

4. Select keepsakes with care. Less doesn't mean none, Becker said. "You don't have to get rid of all your sentimental treasures, but when you own fewer of them, the ones you keep will have greater value." After her grandmother died, Becker's wife wanted to keep many of her grandmother's belongings but eventually came away with only three: her grandmother's favorite candy dish, a brooch, and her Bible. It was enough.

5. Take five to cut ten. Go in your closet, and, in five minutes, remove ten garments you no longer wear or need, and put them in a box for Goodwill. Feeling more ambitious? Try Becker's 333 fashion challenge: Choose thirty-three articles of clothing—not counting undergarments or athletic wear —and stash everything else away. Wear those thirty-three garments exclusively for three weeks. When he hears me gasp in horror, he adds, "People love this exercise more than they think they will."

6. Find a home for everything. Keep your desk, kitchen and bathroom counters, and tabletops clear. Store kitchen appliances out of sight. Put items on your desk in a drawer or file. Throw junk mail away immediately and have a place out of sight for receipts and bills. The key word here is "keep." After you clear once, maintain the habit.

Plain, Simple, Useful Living

In June 2020, I had the honor of interviewing legendary designer Terence Conran. That is, ahem, Sir Terence Orby Conran, to us. At age eighty-eight, he was nearing the end of his accomplished life. A few months after our interview, his devoted secretary e-mailed to let me know of Conran's death and to say mine was the last interview he gave and he'd enjoyed the exchange very much.

Considered one of the world's most influential designers, Conran started a design studio and two international retail chains of home furnishing stores, launched several restaurants, established a publishing house, founded the Design Museum of London, published fifty books, married five women, fathered five children, and had been knighted by Queen Elizabeth II for his contributions to design.

I call that a full life. I'd reached out that June day because a new edition of his classic book *Plain Simple Useful: The Essence of Conran Style* was being released, courtesy of Conran Octopus Publishing.

Given that I stand transfixed at the intersection of beautiful living and prudent spending, I appreciated knowing that, despite his immense wealth, Conran remained deliberately unpretentious. His home and book reflect Quaker-like restraint.

"Objects and surroundings that are plain, simple, and useful are the keys to easy living," he wrote in his introduction. "By grounding us in reality and performing well over time, they are as much the antidote to pointless complexity and superficial styling as they are to the shoddy and second-rate."

Loaded with design basics and punctuated with charming digressions on products he favors and their provenance (the Kilner jar, Duralex glasses, the trestle table), *Plain Simple Useful* holds forth on every room in the house, as well as the yard. Here's a taste:

On kitchens: An appliance that takes longer to clean and reassemble than it does to operate . . . is often more trouble than it's worth. . . . Whatever you display should ideally be used on a regular basis.

On work areas: If utility areas are not scruffy afterthoughts, daily chores will seem less of an imposition. Even the smallest working areas, such as broom cupboards and linen closets, can have a certain down-to-earth charm if they are fitted out with care.

On bedrooms: Nothing should stand between you and a good night's sleep—no distracting clutter, no overflowing wardrobes, no dust-catching knick-knacks. . . . Concentrate on getting the basics right: the quality of light and air, the bed linen that goes next to your skin, and the bed itself.

Because I had questions that went beyond the pages of his book, I reached Conran at his home in the English countryside, where, with the help of his long-time assistant, he fielded my curiosities from across the pond:

What do you wish more people understood about better living?

I have always believed that most people crave simplicity and don't want to live in complex, overly designed homes. That theme runs throughout my book and is more important now than ever in these quite demented times we live in. If I close my eyes and imagine my dream room right now, I'd be sat on a comfortable, well-used sofa with plump cushions, linen curtains fluttering in the breeze from open windows overlooking a wild meadow. Nothing complicated. You don't have to spend vast sums to live a comfortable, happy life.

I love to remind readers that you don't have to be rich to live well. You echo this in your book. What are your top tips for living beautifully without spending much?

I am a child of the Second World War and the subsequent years of rationing, so I am naturally thrifty. Nature will always be generous with her gifts. If you look hard enough, cuttings from the garden will provide flowers for your home most of the year and give you an even greater pleasure than flowers from a store. Likewise, growing your own fruit, vegetables, and herbs is tremendously satisfying.

Natural light is absolutely free, so think of simple ways of flooding a room with it. Candlelight is also very seductive.

Keeping a room tidy, clean, and free of clutter is also a free way to make any interior more pleasant. The key to this is being organized and understanding your home and how it works. Spending time on this will give you an uplifting sense of breathing space.

What is your favorite room in the home and why?

I have always said the kitchen, although I have a terrifically painful back injury at the minute, so the bathroom and the luxury of a hot, deep, and soothing bath runs a very close second. The kitchen though is a terrifically social place at the heart of family life where the joys of cooking, entertaining, drinking and eating can all happily merge.

I hope as you give careful thought to what to put in your right-sized life and to what no longer belongs, you will think of Joshua

Becker and Terence Conran and maybe use their approach to living as a backstop when editing your own belongings and acquiring perhaps a few more. I hope their philosophy will help you make careful, conscious decisions about what to live with, how to live better, and what no longer has a place in your rightsized life.

> Objects and surroundings that are plain, simple, and useful are the keys to easy living. By grounding us in reality and performing well over time, they are as much the antidote to pointless complexity and superficial styling as they are to the shoddy and second-rate.
>
> —Sir Terence Conran

To their good advice, I would add one more recommendation: *make it a lifestyle.* Purge once thoroughly, and then maintain the new order. Don't make downsizing a one-time event. Make it a way of living.

Lighten up, let go, and join me as we go room by room to learn what each room should have so you can live better now.

THE KITCHEN

Let's Get Cooking!

*Always start out with a larger pot
than you think you need.*
—Julia Child

Everyone knows the kitchen is the heart and soul of any home. It draws us in with its good smells, good meals, good conversation, and good memories. But it's also a clutter trap when we fill it with cookware and gadgets that overtake this hardworking space and don't pull their weight. Let's look at the absolute essentials to equip your kitchen once and right, from linens and pans that improve over time, to glassware and knives that do their job better than their competitors, plus what every kitchen *doesn't* need.

In our efforts to become top chefs, at least in our own domains, we often think that buying more cookware and novelty appliances will help. If you think kitchen stuff is going to turn you into Julia Child, you're only half right.

Your cookware does have a significant impact on the quality of your cooking. However, you do not need as much as you think. In the kitchen, as well as in other areas of the house, more is not better. Better is better. Too much equipment backfires and gets in the way of you and the perfect tool. Knowing what to buy and what to keep and editing out extraneous items will help you make the best use of precious kitchen space and make you a more efficient cook.

Let's get a handle on tea towels, flatware, pans, wineglasses, and knives.

CHAPTER 16

Give the Humble Tea Towel Its Rightful Due

As long as humans have had kitchens, we've had kitchen towels. Once made from feed bags, flour sacks, or animal skins, kitchen cloths have evolved handsomely over the centuries. This is fortunate, as few of us go through a single day without grabbing one. And so, our journey toward outfitting our homes once and right starts in the kitchen with this most humble servant: the tea towel.

Most kitchens have a drawer full of these. Some do their job better than others—and we will explore why. Some are so pretty they can double as décor but don't work well.

My litmus test for any household staple is that it excels in both function and form. That is, it looks good and works perfectly.

We expect our kitchen towels to dry dishes, wipe counters, line baskets, cover baked goods, all while sitting out and looking pretty. But what else should we expect from these little workhorses? I want a kitchen towel that is highly absorbent, dries quickly between uses, lasts for years, gets better with age, doesn't leave behind streaks or lint as it wipes, and that adds a touch of style, personality, or whimsy to the kitchen.

Dish towels or tea towels can be made of linen, cotton, or a blend of both. If it's terrycloth, it can be a dish towel but technically, not a tea towel.

I learned this and other fine points of the tea towel from textile historian Marnie Fogg, author of *The Art of the Tea Towel* (Batsford Books, November 2018). Colorful printed tea towels began brightening kitchens as part of the post-World-War-II euphoria, she told me. Since then, artists have designed tea towels featuring a wide range of subjects: castles, teapots, foxes, nutcrackers, the royals, farm animals, and sayings: *Many hands make light work*, just as a tiny sampling. What I love about this historical progression is how business and artistry combined to elevate an everyday household item to literally putting good design in the hands of everyone.

Until I spoke to Fogg, I had always viewed tea towels as whimsical souvenirs brought home to remind me of fun places I'd visited. I didn't know to look for a qualitative difference or even what those differences were. But now I do.

"I don't like going through life not thinking about details," she said. "If you are going to do something, anything, whether you're making a meal or setting a table, do it beautifully."

Amen.

What to Look for When Buying a Tea Towel

To raise the refinement level in your rightsized home, here are some of the finer points of choosing tea towels.

- **Look for linen.** One-hundred percent linen tea towels are the gold standard. Second best are cotton-linen blends. "Linen union" is a blend of 55 percent linen and 45 percent cotton. Pure cotton tea towels are most common but don't perform nearly as well as linen. Pass those by and definitely avoid cotton terry dish towels. They are bulky to store, stay soggy, and trap crumbs and particles so are less hygienic.

- **Linen beats cotton not only for its strength and long-wearing nature but also because it won't leave lint behind when used for drying and it won't pill.** Linen is coarser, stronger, and more breathable than cotton and gets better with age; cotton wears out faster. I have one Irish linen tea towel I purchased forty years ago. It has been in my regular lineup, far outlasting all the cotton towels purchased since.

- **Shop beyond the souvenir shops.** Look for Irish or Belgian linen, the two best linens in the world, at nicer housewares or linen stores. Linen from China is often not as good; it's thinner and wrinkles more.

- **Assess the design.** To take your tea towels to the next level, find a store or company that specializes in designer-inspired lines and begin to view these household servants as art. Because towels are often out of their drawers and visible, pick designs as if you were picking out clothing for your kitchen. What should it wear to look good?

- **Give your tea towel drawer a makeover.** Replace cotton dishtowels with pure linen ones in designs that delight you.

"Most of us don't have to deal with large matters every day," Fogg said, "but we all have to deal with little things every day. We need to respect the things we live with."

And that includes our tea towels.

Lessons in Linen

Though often used interchangeably, linen and cotton are quite different fabrics. For starters, they come from different plants. Linen comes from flax plants, one of the oldest cultivated plants in human history. Cotton comes from cotton plants. Fibers used to make linen come from flax stalks. These linen fibers are thicker and longer than those made from cotton, which is spun from the bolls, or seed hairs, of cotton plants. Linen is humble and durable and mixes well with wood, metal, other fabrics, and all décor styles. Besides making the best tea towels, linen makes excellent bedding, tablecloths, and napkins, and heavier-weight linen works well for drapery and slipcovers.

And, no, you don't have to iron it. While a pile of ironed tea towels looks nice in a stack or in a drawer, some believe linen's rumpled nature, how it looks straight from the dryer, is part of its charm.

Caring for Your Tea Towels

Although our tea towels get used and abused, wash them with kindness. Use eco-friendly laundry soap and water no hotter than warm. If they get stains, presoak them in a stronger soap solution. Avoid chlorine bleach and air dry when possible. "I do iron them all," Fogg said. "Don't just stick them rumpled in the drawer." Hmmm, I'll leave that up to you. But ironed towels do look nice, and since talking to Fogg, I have gotten in the habit of ironing mine. (See tips on how to iron cotton and linen in Chapter 22.)

Summary: Choosing Tea Towels

- Buy 100 percent linen.

- Shop beyond the souvenir shops at nicer housewares or linen stores.

- Select designs as if picking out clothing for your kitchen.

- Look for Irish or Belgian linen.

CHAPTER 17

Finding Flatware
That's a Cut Above

Now here's something to chew on. What common household item do you hold and put in your mouth fifty times a day? That's more than your toothbrush. And when was the last time you thought about it?

I hadn't paid my flatware much attention since I bought it thirty years ago. It just sat in the drawer, waiting to transport food to my mouth, which I appreciated. But when I discovered I had half as many forks as knives, I took notice. *What happened?* I started out with the same number of each.

"The forks ran away with the spoons!" I cried to Greg Owens, co-owner of Sherrill Manufacturing, which makes Liberty Tabletop flatware, the only flatware still made in America.

Owens, who unlike me, actually does give flatware a lot of thought, had heard this before. "Forks and spoons often get lost to trash cans, lunch sacks, picnics, and camping trips," he said.

MARNI MANTRA:
Buy it once,
buy it right.

"Apart from what you may have filched from the college cafeteria, flatware is one of those purchases you typically only make twice in your life," Owens said. Secretly, I was glad to have the excuse to do this again, and to buy it once more and buy it right.

How to Pick Cutlery That Makes the Cut

As I began shopping for something I hadn't bought in thirty years, and likely won't ever buy again, I researched what I should look for. Here's what I learned makes the cutlery cut:

- **Material.** The key factor in choosing quality stainless-steel flatware is to look at the metal content. The back usually has a stamp that reads 18/10, 18/8, or 18/0. This ratio represents the amount of chromium to nickel in the metal mix or alloy. Nickel (the second number) gives utensils luster and durability, and reduces their susceptibility to pitting, rusting, clouding, and staining. The higher the nickel content, the better the flatware. Because nickel is expensive, many manufacturers skimp on it. But now you know better. Avoid any flatware stamped 18/0, in favor of 18/10 flatware, or at least 18/8.

- **Production quality.** Judge flatware by its finish. Pieces should have an even luster with no pitting, no irregular pattern detailing, and no areas that appear worn or overbuffed. Look between the fork tines. An inferior product will show roughness there.

- **Style.** Flatware designs fall into three categories: modern (sleek and streamlined), traditional (floral designs, ornate flourishes, or curves), and decorative (hammered, stippled, or woven effects). The smoother the finish and the simpler the pattern, the more it will show fingerprints, dings and scratches. That's not necessarily bad. Patterned handles hide scratches and dings so tend to hold onto their newness longer. Avoid colored, non-metallic handles, which tend to be less durable.

- **Size.** Flatware size falls into two camps: American Standard and European. American Standard flatware is typically an inch smaller than European-sized pieces. An American Standard fork measures about seven inches long, while its European counterpart measures eight inches. Though some US consumers still prefer traditional American sizing, the trend is toward less ornate, larger, and heavier pieces, known in the industry as Euro-sizing. To know what you prefer, try before you buy.

- **Feel.** When selecting the flatware you will hold every day, pay attention to how it feels in your hand. Pick up a piece and get a sense of its balance, weight, and contours. Of the four styles my husband and I ordered to test, one we eliminated because the sides of the handle were square and felt sharp against our fingers. Contours should feel pleasant to hold. Heft is also important. Utensils should feel balanced in your hand and not tumble forward or back. Because flatware is one item you need to see and feel in person, if you plan to order online, order samples to try first.

- **Strength.** You don't want your flatware to feel like the flimsy stuff found in school cafeterias. "It should pass the ice cream test," Owens said. "You should be able to scoop hard ice cream without bending the spoon."

- **Compatibility.** Your flatware and dishware need to get along. Set each pattern you're considering alongside your china and everyday dishes to see how they work together. Some patterns fight. Usually, if your dishes are simple, your silverware can be more ornate, though plain also works. Conversely, a patterned plate may look better with simpler flatware.

- **Hollow or solid?** The world of flatware has two types of knife handles. Neither is inherently better, but be aware of the difference. Hollow-handled knives are formed when two halves of the handle come together around the tang of the blade. Cutlery makers solder the halves together and fill the hollow with epoxy or cement. They often feel more balanced so are less likely to fall off the edge of a plate. In solid-handle knife construction, makers forge knives out of one solid piece of steel, which makes knives stronger.

Caring for Your Cutlery

To keep your cutlery gleaming for years, proper handling is important. Don't dump your flatware in a sink with a hundred other pieces banging around. That will scratch it. When putting it in the dishwasher, use trays or cutlery baskets that separate pieces.

Summary: Choosing Stainless Flatware

- **Material:** Look for metal stamp of 18/10.

- **Feel:** Utensils should feel balanced and comfortable in your hand.

- **Strength:** You should be able to scoop hard ice cream without bending the teaspoon.

- **Style:** Smooth is beautiful but may show nicks and dings that patterned handles hide.

- **Test:** Try before you buy. If you plan to order online, order samples first.

CHAPTER 18

Can the Right Pots and Pans Make You a Better Cook? *Yes!*

F or more years than I would like to say, my relationship with pans went like this, "Oh, this is a pan. It will work." I had little to no regard for the differences among pans other than size.

But one night, as I was cooking meatballs, that changed. I was making the same meatballs I had made dozens of times. I buy them premade from the grocery store and cook them in a skillet for twenty-five minutes. I turn them so they brown on all sides, then pour a jar of premade spaghetti sauce on them, and let them simmer. Nothing complicated.

Now, although I had made these same meatballs before, this time after just a few seconds, they were instantly black on one side, not brown. *What the heck?* The only difference between this night and the dozens of other times I'd cooked these meatballs was that I'd grabbed a different skillet. This tripped the what-don't-I-know lightbulb, which is how most of my journalistic inquiries begin.

I called up America's Test Kitchen, a company devoted to making home cooks feel more confident by teaching cooking basics through public TV shows and magazines. I talked to Lisa McManus, executive editor of America's Test Kitchen reviews, who reassured me, "It's not you. It's the pan."

"How do you know?" I asked.

"You've made this recipe before successfully, and the pan is the only factor that changed," said McManus, whose job involves cooking the same recipes in different pans to find out which cookware performs better and why.

"Everyone can cook," she said. "But often home cooks have a bad experience, blame themselves, and give up. It's not their fault. They're ill-equipped. Their cookware lets them down."

I love this woman.

"Your pan should be your partner, not your adversary."

Then McManus gave me a crash course in cookware and assured me better meals were just a pan away. Since my meatball moment, I've done more investigating and made a few key discoveries and purchases. As a result, I am the same cook, with better pans.

Here again a little knowledge will make your money go further, your investment last longer, your rightsized kitchen more efficient, and your meals better. Moreover, if you get the right pans, you can let go of the wrong ones, as you'll likely have the better ones for the rest of your life. Let's look at what makes a great pan.

Know Your Metals

To understand how a pan performs, you need to get a handle on how various metals used to make pans interact with heat. Most cookware is made of stainless steel, aluminum, cast iron, its cousin carbon steel, copper, or a combination. Each metal has distinct properties related to how it conducts and distributes heat. Here's the rundown:

Copper is the Ferrari in the kitchen, fast to react, expensive, and high maintenance. Though its responsiveness has made it a favorite among top chefs, for most cooks it's overkill. It's costly and requires care and polishing beyond most people's patience. It also can react to acidic foods, like tomatoes, changing food's flavor.

Aluminum is the next best heat conductor, and far less expensive, making it popular in fast-food restaurants, where chefs want to turn food out lightning quick. Like copper, aluminum can also react to acidic foods. So you don't want this pan for your spaghetti sauce. A soft metal, aluminum scratches and dents easily.

Stainless steel is "the bomb," experts say, and what you find in most homes. It's stable, resists corrosion, and won't react to acidic foods. For overall versatility and price, stainless steel cookware tops the list. However, you have to know how to cook in a stainless-steel pan. To prevent food from sticking, start with food that is room temperature. Heat the pan, and then add oil or butter to the hot pan; add food when the fat is hot.

Because stainless steel has poor heat conductivity, food can cook unevenly. To fix that, manufacturers developed three-ply or five-ply pans, which have stainless-steel surfaces with a layer of aluminum or copper sandwiched in between. This provides the heat conductivity of aluminum or copper and the strength and stability of stainless.

Three-ply does the job. The five-ply and copper-core pans cost more but aren't that much better.

Cast iron has been used in cookware since before the Middle Ages. Cooks swear by it. Cast iron is extremely durable, provides excellent heat retention, and is inexpensive. With proper care, a cast-iron pan can last a lifetime or longer. It improves with age, but you do need to keep these pans "seasoned" by wiping them with a light coating of oil after each use to create a natural nonstick surface and prevent rust, or they, too, will react to acidic foods.

Carbon steel offers the same benefits of cast iron but is lighter—though still heavier than stainless steel—and more expensive than both. It, too, gets better with age and needs seasoning, like its cast-iron cousin.

Deciding whether you want stainless steel, cast iron, copper, aluminum, or a combination depends on how much time you spend cooking, your expertise in the kitchen, and your budget. However, since pans play a significant role in the kitchen and take up a lot of space, you want each one to pull its weight.

In the test kitchen, pan tests involve making the same recipe over and over in many pans of the same size from different makers to see what works and what annoys. "If I am fighting the pan and burning my hand, it's not working," McManus said.

Once you know the pan essentials, plus the pans that are nice to have, you have permission to get rid of those under-used, under-performing, under-the-counter cloggers. Ten crummy pans do not equal one great one. Every pan in your kitchen should do its job exceptionally and should be your ally, not your adversary, when you cook. Here's to hoping you and your pans make beautiful meals together.

The Four Core Pieces Every Well-Equipped Kitchen Needs

In talking with McManus further, I learned that, although my kitchen contained plenty of cookware, it was in fact ill-equipped. I did not have the right basic pans, and what I did have was subpar. Though I name a few brands below that ATK recommends, what's important is not the brand so much as that you know the kitchen basics as well as properties to look for and avoid:

- **A Dutch oven.** These high-sided, cast-iron, enamel-coated cookers can go from stovetop to oven and can be used to steam, deep fry, braise, stew, bake, or roast. Choose round shapes over oval because round fits burners better. Start with the seven-quart size because, while a large pot can accommodate less food, a smaller one cannot hold more. Cooks universally agree that Le Creuset makes the winning Dutch oven, but it's expensive. A best buy runner-up is the less expensive Cuisinart Chef's Classic Enameled Dutch Oven Casserole.

- **A large four-quart saucepan with lid.** A high-walled saucepan that can handle gravies, soups, and puddings is another kitchen must. At ATK, the category winner is the All-Clad tri-ply stainless saucepan. Again, start large, and get smaller saucepans later.

- **A twelve-inch stainless-steel skillet.** This is the hardest worker in the kitchen. Again, although this book is not brand driven, when the jury comes in with comments like this from the *New York Times*, consumers should know: "After more than seventy collective hours of research and testing . . . we still think the tri-ply All-Clad stainless twelve-inch covered fry pan is the best skillet for the money (around $120). It's a durable pan that heats extremely evenly . . . Yes, it's expensive, but we think it's worth the money considering it will last a lifetime."

- **A twelve-inch, cast-iron skillet, or carbon steel skillet.** Lodge makes the winning cast-iron skillet. This is the one pan to get if you're short on cash, space, or both. I found a Lodge twelve-inch cast-iron pan at Home Goods for fifteen dollars. My fried chicken is finally as good as my Aunt Edith's—which she made in her black iron skillet. In the carbon steel category, the ATK team favorite is the Matfer Bourgeat Black Steel round frying pan. We bought a twelve-inch, carbon-steel pan from de Buyer that has worked out well. When properly cared for and seasoned, both cast iron and carbon steel develop nonstick surfaces naturally and never need replacing.

- **Nice to have.** After you have this four-piece core set, the following items fall into the would-be-nice-to-have category: A generous stockpot (eight to twelve quarts), a two-quart saucepan, a ten-inch skillet, an eight-inch skillet, and a nonstick skillet for delicate foods, like fish and eggs.

Although I had a dozen pots and pans, of the four essential pieces every kitchen should have, I

> But often home cooks have a bad experience, blame themselves and give up. It's not their fault. They're ill-equipped. Their cookware lets them down.
>
> —Lisa McManus

had only two. The four pans I did use most often were the Teflon-coated, nonstick variety, not a chef's first choice. The surface of a nonstick pan only lasts a few years, and mine were going on ten. Of the four essentials, I lacked a Dutch oven and a cast-iron skillet. I fixed that. I also did away with the pans I never used that were hogging space, and now rely on my Le Creuset, my Lodge cast iron, and my de Buyer. Dinners are markedly better.

Dos and Don'ts of Pan Purchasing

Because good pans are both a household staple and an investment, home cooks should buy and build a core collection with care, while heeding the cautions below:

- **Don't buy a set.** Cookware sets are full of pieces you don't need that take up space. Retailers like to sell sets because they can offer twenty-one pieces for $199, but most people never use half the pieces, and those extras will clog up kitchen cupboards, which we're not going to do in our rightsized home. Having matching pans is not important. Having pans that work is.

- **Do buy pans one at a time based on what you cook and can afford.** Start with a few durable, flexible workhorses that will earn their keep, and build.

- **Don't fall for celebrity brands.** Celebrity chefs don't make cookware; they build brands. When kitchenware companies ask celebrity chefs to lend their names to a cookware line, it's not really what the celebrity has expertise in. It's just marketing.

- **Do buy pans from well-established cookware companies** that only make cookware.

- **Don't buy a pan without holding it.** How a pan feels in your hand is important.

- **Do get the right grip.** Try lifting the pan by the handle and see if you can turn it without it slipping. Look for metal handles that can go from stove to oven.

- **Don't make nonstick pans your first purchase.** Although nonstick pans are easy to clean and inexpensive, the coating goes downhill fast, so they need to be replaced every few years. With wear, the coating, usually made of polytetrafluoroethylene, or PTFE, (popularly known as Teflon), blisters, peels, and gets into the food you're cooking and eating, which has raised health concerns.

- **Do start your recipe with a little oil in a regular pan.** That said, McManus likes to keep one nonstick pan around for cooking eggs and frying fish.

Caring for Your Cookware

Now, that I've likely cost you some money on new pans, the least I can do is make this investment last the rest of your life. Here's how:

- **Handwash.** Dishwashers are harsh environments. Though the manufacturer may say its pans are dishwasher safe, putting pans in the dishwasher will accelerate their demise and could warp them.

- **Cool it.** Do not rush your hot pan into cold water. Thermal shock is hard on metal. Once your pan is cool enough to touch, wash it in warm water. Similarly, don't throw a cold pan on a high flame. Let it warm up gradually.

- **Embrace the grunge.** Pans are not décor items (unless you're one of those who hangs your polished copper cookware over the stove). Cookware should look used. Just as you don't want the carpenter with the hammer that looks brand new, you don't want a chef with shiny new pans. However, if you want to restore some original shine, mix Bar Keepers Friend with water to make a paste, and scour. Bar Keepers Friend is a good all-around cleaner for pots and pans, ovens and sinks.

- **Stained enamel?** Though enamel-coated pans, like those in a Dutch oven, won't acquire seasoning like uncoated cast iron, their light surfaces can darken. To restore them, make a solution of one-part bleach and three parts water, and let the mixture soak in the pan overnight.

- **The beauty of stainless-steel pans,** which often have a core of aluminum, is their durability. Handwash them with soap; soak them overnight if you need to, and scrub all you want with a plastic scrubber. Steel scrubbers can scratch the surface.

Cast-iron and carbon-steel pans

- **These pans need to be seasoned.** This means creating a coating of oil and fat, so when the pan heats, it has a naturally nonstick surface. For pans that don't come pre-seasoned, or that need reseasoning, here's how: Wash the pan in warm water. Let it dry completely. Spread a thin layer of melted shortening or oil over it. Put it in a 400-degree oven on a rack upside down. Put a baking sheet underneath to catch drips. Bake for one hour. Cool and wipe.

- **Go easy on the soap.** When washing cast-iron or carbon-steel pans, let them cool, and then rinse and scrub with a brush or plastic scrubber. Soap can strip away the seasoning. But if the pan is well seasoned, a little soap won't hurt.

- **Don't soak.** If food is stuck on these pans, use boiling water to loosen it. Rinse, dry, and set it back on the warm burner to finish drying. Don't soak these pans overnight; soaking cast iron or carbon steel breaks down the oils you want to preserve.

- **Reseason.** Once the pan is dry, add a drop of any kind of cooking oil, about the size of half a dime. Wipe it all over the pan. If your pan ever feels sticky or gummy, it has too much oil. Then you will need soap to get the gunk off, and reseason. Regularly adding just the thinnest coat will keep the pan perfect.

- **Rust is okay.** If your cast-iron or carbon-steel pans get rusty, no problem. Just scrub the rust off with water, wipe, oil, and start over. You can't hurt these pans.

Summary: Choosing Pots and Pans

- Know your metals.

- Start with four basic pieces: Dutch oven, four-quart saucepan, twelve-inch skillet, twelve-inch cast iron skillet.

- Avoid sets and celebrity brands.

CHAPTER 19

The One-and-Done Wineglass

I f the last time you went out to buy wineglasses, you came home with a five-alarm headache and a bag of plastic tumblers, you, like me, have probably asked yourself: Why, WHY are there so many kinds of wineglasses? Do we really need a different glass for every variety of wine—one for chardonnay, another for pinot noir, one for cabernet, and another for dessert wine?

Holy Haut Medoc! you think. Who has that kind of shelf space?

I decided to get to the bottom of this oak barrel. Now, I have this belief that when you cross the half-century mark in age, you should know these things, yet I hadn't the vaguest idea. So I summoned Gabe Geller, a top sommelier at Royal Wine Corp., a 150-year-old producer, importer, and exporter of wines and spirits based in Bayonne, New Jersey, and asked, "How many types of wineglasses does a home really need?"

"The world of wineglasses can seem intimidating," Geller said. "Some companies design a different glass for every type of wine. It's a bit of a marketing shtick."

"Thank you!" I said.

"Realistically, one good universal wineglass is perfectly suitable for anything, from your summer afternoon white to your complex heavy red."

"Cheers to that!"

Though he appreciates the research and testing that go into the different shapes, he concedes, only the effete few will notice or care. And if your friends are judging, you need new friends.

"Most people don't have the room or budget for a variety of shapes and sizes, so having that many different glasses is impractical," said Geller.

We rightsizers are paying attention!

"You will do fine sticking with one universal wineglass," he said, adding that he wants to demystify the wineglass "so people can spend more time enjoying their wine and less time worrying about the vessel."

Properties of the Universal Wineglass

In keeping with my mantra *buy it once, buy it right*, I wanted to know more about this one-size-fits-all wineglass, which works for white, rosé, and red wine. (Okay, one exception: to properly serve Champagne, spring for some fluted glasses.) Here's what to look for:

- **The just-right size.** The universal wineglass should hold thirteen ounces to the brim. If a glass is too big, you lose some aroma; too narrow, and it won't capture the bouquet. A thirteen-ounce glass leaves enough "nose room" for a four-to-six-ounce pour.

- **A pear shape.** The perfect, all-around glass should be broader at the bowl's base than at the rim. The bowl shape brings out the aromas, which get diffused then brought together as the glass narrows. "Smelling the wine is the most important part of tasting wine," Geller said. "If you lose on aroma, you lose on taste."

- **Pick stems.** Though stemless wineglasses have become trendy, and are practical poolside or for picnics, avoid them for your all-purpose wineglass. Glasses without stems force you to hold the bowl, which leaves fingerprints, doesn't let you see the wine as well, and warms the wine, which you want to keep at serving temperature.

- **Keep it clear.** Although colored and etched glasses might look novel, they will take away from the appearance of the wine, which you want to see to appreciate. Keep glasses clear.

- **Make that crystal clear.** As long as you're only buying one set, splurge on crystal. (This doesn't mean cut crystal.) To be considered crystal, glass must have at least 24 percent lead content, which allows it to be thinner and clearer. Thick glass impairs your ability to see the wine clearly. One way to determine if a glass is crystal is to gently tap it with a metal spoon. If you hear a long, high-pitched ping, it's crystal. A short-lived clunk indicates glass.

- **Avoid speed bumps.** A good wineglass also has a thin lip. Lower-quality glasses have thick rims with a bump around the edge. Avoid these. That speed bump on the lip gets in the way and impedes sipping flow.

Caring for Your Wineglasses

Some wine purists believe in washing wineglasses with only water. Soap can leave a residue that will affect the taste, they argue. Some compromise and wash only the outside of the glass with soap, not the inside. Personally, I'm a fan of soap and water. My advice is wash by hand with a mild detergent, rinse twice. You don't want that first aroma to carry overtones of lemon-scented Joy. Hand dry without twisting from the base, so you don't risk breaking the stem from the bowl. When storing glasses, don't set them upside down, that can chip the precious thin rim and trap odors.

Summary: An All-Purpose Wineglass

- Should hold thirteen ounces to the brim.

- Should be pear-shaped, with a stem, and made of clear, thin crystal.

- Should not have a lumpy rim.

CHAPTER 20

Knives: Cutting
to the Chase

A kitchen without a knife is not a kitchen.
—Masaharu Morimoto, Iron Chef

One day, not long after my pan epiphany, a good friend gave my husband and me an unexpected gift: a chef's knife.

A knife? I was puzzled.

Perhaps he'd heard my pan parable and correctly assumed that my other kitchenware also needed an upgrade, starting with that most basic and essential tool: the chef's knife.

"I love this knife," our friend Bud raved about the Shun Classic Santoku knife. "It will change your life."

Or end it, I thought. Man, was this sharp. Though I had sharpened my old kitchen knives periodically, this knife's edge was in another league.

The first night I tried out my new knife, I slipped it out of its paper sleeve like a Samurai warrior. The dish I was making called for a diced onion and sliced mushrooms. *Whoosh, whoosh.* The knife slid through like Luke Skywalker's lightsaber. Onion juice did not spurt out. Mushrooms didn't mush. *Hmmm*, I was already a better cook.

Although I'd heard that good kitchen knives are the foundation of a well-equipped kitchen, as with so many lessons learned late in life, I didn't really know how important until I felt the contrast firsthand.

This home-chef moment made me want to know more about what makes a great knife great. As the single most-handled item in the kitchen, maybe in the entire house, the kitchen knife gets held even more than the TV remote. Any way you slice it, almost every dish involves cutting something—a tomato, a lemon, nuts, an onion, and ideally not your finger.

Because the chef's knife is so essential, many reviewers have diced the finer points of a variety of chef's knives available on today's market to find which one stands a cut above.

I turned, once again, to Lisa McManus, who with her America's Test Kitchen team has reviewed dozens of knives over twenty years. To evaluate that all-important chef's knife, they asked testers of all sizes, those with large hands and small, male and female, experienced cooks and novices, to put the knives through four universal tasks: they minced fresh herbs (aiming to create confetti, not mush), diced an onion, cut up a butternut squash (a notoriously hard object), and cut a whole chicken into parts.

The result: no one knife is tops in every cook's book. For various reasons, reviewers selected favorites from a variety of manufacturers:

Wüsthof, J.A. Henckels, Global, Misen, Miyabi, Shun, Victorinox, MAC, Mercer. I'm surely forgetting some.

"That's because it's highly personal," McManus said. "What fits you might not fit me."

When you do get your hands on that perfect knife, you know. "It feels like magic," she said, "like an extension of you. It flies into your hand, feels comfortable, and fits. It doesn't slip. It feels natural and balanced."

Best Knife Tips

Here's what to know when picking your rightsized kitchen knives for life:

- **Avoid the block set.** As with pans, don't buy a blocked knife set. They may look nice on the counter, and may have one or two good knives, but they have a lot of fill. Instead, buy knives individually, and not necessarily from the same maker.

- **You only need three.** Cooking pros agree, just three knives can do every job in the kitchen. The king is the eight-inch chef's knife, the go-to for cutting meat, fish, herbs, produce, nuts, you name it. Next, invest in a good, long (ten-inch), serrated knife, for cutting through crusty bread and items with differing layers of resistance, like sandwiches. Finally, a good three-to-four-inch paring knife is a must when you need precision and control cutting, or for coring small items, like strawberries. Once you have those essentials, you should be set. However, if you have the space and inclination, consider adding a boning knife, or a six-inch chef's knife.

- **Mind the metal.** Knowing what makes a great blade involves a deep dive into the science of metallurgy. We're not going there, but here's the upshot. How the steel comes together determines a knife's strength and performance. Stainless steel knives are most popular. Some chefs swear by carbon steel knives, which get high marks for performance, but, unlike stainless, will discolor.

- **German or Japanese?** A discussion of knives doesn't get far before a debate over East–West virtues surfaces. German knives (such as Wüsthof and J.A. Henckels) are known for sturdiness and strength. Heavier and thicker, their blades work more like an ax or wedge. Because they dull faster, they require more frequent sharpening. Japanese knives (such as Shun, Miyabi) are made of harder steel, so they can be thinner and thus sharper. Known for their razor-like precision (think cutting sashimi), Japanese knives stay sharper longer. But being harder makes them more brittle and prone to chipping.

- **Get a grip.** As important as blade strength, sharpness, and longevity is grip. You want a handle that offers what ergonomic experts call "affordance," the ability to shift your grip, rather than force your hand into a specific hold. Texture is also important. In the kitchen, hands get wet and greasy, so you want a handle that won't slip and become unsafe.

- **Tang and bolster.** Knife shopping inevitably turns up words like stamped, forged, tang, and bolster. Stamped means the knife blades were punched cookie-cutter like out of a sheet of steel. A forged knife involves crafting one blade at a time, which makes forged knives more expensive and a favorite of aficionados. Tang is how far the blade metal extends into the handle. Through to the end is desirable. A knife's tang will affect its balance, how its weight falls in your hand. The bolster is where the blade meets the handle. Look for a smooth union that won't let food and bacteria get trapped in the joint. The space between the bottom of the bolster and the bottom heel of the blade should allow enough room for your knuckles.

- **It's not about price.** ATK reviewed knives ranging from $25 to $300 and found price did not always equal quality. Some of the best performers were surprisingly affordable, while those that cost much more truly didn't cut it. In fact, their top performers in the above categories were as follows: Victorinox Swiss Army Fibrox Pro eight-inch (around $40); Mercer ten-to-twelve-inch serrated knife (around $23); Victorinox three-and-one-quarter-inch paring knife (around $8).

Caring for Your Knives

Although chefs don't all agree on the best knife, they agree on this: the best knife is the sharpest one. A great knife with a dull edge will never be better than an inferior knife that is razor sharp. And no knife stays sharp forever; all need sharpening.

"If it's not sharp, you might as well use a letter opener," said Gregg Kurtz, a professional knife sharpener for forty-five years. "Sharp knives are safer because they go where you want them to and don't slide out of control. A sharp edge also makes food look and taste better. Dull knives make messy cuts, crush food, and leave flavor on the cutting board."

Between professional sharpenings, maintain knife edges at home up by running them along a knife honer. Lay the blade's beveled surface against the honing rod and run it the length of the hone on one side and then the other. It won't sharpen the blade but will straighten the edge, which gets bent with use. Electric knife sharpeners, which Lisa McManus favors for their convenience, are another option, but use them correctly, or you may grind away too much metal.

To keep edges sharp longer, never cut into frozen food, or on glass or stone. Cut on wooden or plastic cutting boards. Store knives in a wooden block or on a magnetic strip, not loose in a drawer. Handwash them. Avoid putting them in the dishwasher as this can warp the wood. Sharpen them regularly.

"If you start with good knives, and take care of them, you will have them for life," Kurtz said.

Summary: Choosing Kitchen Knives

- The three essential kitchen knives are an eight-inch chef's knife, a ten-inch serrated knife, and a good three-to-four-inch paring knife.

- Don't buy a blocked set.

- Both German and Japanese knives, though different, have their strengths.

- Look for a blade with a tang that extends all the way through the handle.

The Stuff of Dreams

There are three things that always look very beautiful to me: my same good pair of old shoes that don't hurt, my own bedroom, and US Customs on the way back home.
—Andy Warhol, American artist

Mantra: *The closer something is to your body, the better it should be.* And what gets closer than our bedding? In these upcoming chapters, we will deconstruct the bed by layer, so as you outfit your rightsized home, you will know how to build the best nest for rest. We'll pull the covers off the mattress industry, cut through the thread-count hype, and get the lowdown on down. All so every bit of bedding in your rightsized home delivers exceptional comfort and a soft landing. Come, let's build your dreamy bedroom.

CHAPTER 21

Mattress Matters

N o matter how pretty your bedroom is, the part you can't see—your mattress—has a bigger impact on your sleep quality than anything else in the room. It's also one of the most expensive items in the room, with the average consumer spending $1,000 on a queen-size mattress with box spring, and some as much as $5,000.

I stumbled into the mattress underworld after going on a business trip where I woke up in a nice hotel and had the oddest sensation. As I got out of bed, my lower back, which, when I get up, usually feels like someone poured concrete down my vertebral column and it hardened, felt as loose as a licorice rope.

That's odd, I thought. *My back feels great. I must have slept funny.* But the second night at the same hotel, it happened again.

On this second promising morning of waking up feeling half my age, I tore back the sheets to reveal the label of this wonder mattress.

Though the name is not important, it was a Sealy Posturepedic Plush Euro Pillowtop custom labeled for this hotel. I snapped a picture of the label with my phone.

Back home, I pulled back the covers to see what I'd been sleeping on. It was a Sears-O-Pedic Solace Pillowtop, circa World War II, judging from its sagging sides. No wonder!

This mattress was officially an ex-mattress.

Next, I went undercover to find out how to make this big, important purchase right. I learned it's a squishy business. Prices seem arbitrary. Most sales are final, so you're stuck. And, unlike buying a washing machine or a lawnmower, where most consumers want the same qualities, mattresses are highly personal, so consumer reviews and reports are almost useless.

Say Yes to the Rest

I spoke to representatives from Tempur Sealy, the world's leading mattress manufacturer; from the Better Sleep Council, the education arm of the International Sleep Products Association; from Good-Beds.com, a mattress matchmaking and clearinghouse; and to an orthopedic spine surgeon. I read current consumer trend data, and the few, small, published studies on the subject.

I factored all that into my own experience, including trading in my old mattress for the hotel model, and here, to echo Oprah Winfrey, is what I know for sure:

Mattresses are not one size fits all. What works for me may not work for you. Your one star may be my five star. So don't pick based on what I, your brother, or your neighbor likes.

Sleep on it. Lying on a mattress in a retail store is not the best way to choose. A study out of Duke University found that invariably the mattress consumers liked in a showroom was not the one that gave them the best night's sleep. Researchers set seven unlabeled unidentifiable mattress sets in a mock showroom and invited 128 participants to shop for the one that felt best. They could take as much time as they liked. (Most took between ten and fifteen minutes.) Afterward, the participants sleep-tested the seven mattresses in their homes for several weeks, while researchers measured their actigraphic motion, or how often they stirred. (Less tossing equaled better sleep.) Every participant got matched to a mattress that provided the best sleep. However, in almost every case, that mattress was not the one they chose to buy in the showroom. In short, the typical showroom experience did not lead to shoppers choosing the best mattress for them.

The best way to know if a mattress is for you is to sleep on it. If you have a great night's sleep while staying in a hotel or at a friend's, that's a better test. If you wake up feeling better than you do at home, look at the mattress label and take a picture. If that happens in a hotel, note the room number. Hotels often have more than one type of mattress. Many hotels offer a way to order the mattress you slept on through them.

Age factor. Almost any new mattress is better than any old mattress. The biggest difference between a hotel and a home mattress is usually age. Hotels replace their mattresses frequently, often every seven years. They often feel great because you likely won't ever sleep on a worn-out one. Evaluate your mattress every seven years, replace before ten. To find out how old your mattress is, check the tag, that flimsy one that is only to be removed by the customer. It should state the year the mattress was made.

Hotel quality. Because mattresses are the most important furnishing in a hotel room, hotels choose with great care. Just as furnishings made for commercial settings are stronger than those for residential use, hotel mattresses are designed for more punishment. Manufacturers use commercial-grade foam, which is denser and more resilient. Mattress covers, ticking, and inner springs will all be higher gauge. The foundations, or box springs, will typically provide stronger support, and hotel mattress edges are sturdier and straighter. Residential mattresses have a softer, even slightly rounded edge. At home, if you sleep close to the edge of your mattress, you risk rolling off. On a hotel bed, you can sleep up to the edge.

Find your fit and feel. Do you prefer bounce or squish? Some people like to sink into a bed and have it hug them like a cradle. They think memory-foam mattresses are the stuff of dreams. Others think those mattresses feel like quicksand, and prefer to float on their mattress, to sleep on it rather than in it. Because every body is different, look for a mattress that suits your curves, weight, size, shape, and preferred sleep position (stomach, side, or back). If you share your bed, be sure to find one that suits your partner, too.

Bells and whistles. Adjustable bed bases, where consumers can make the feet or head of the bed go up or down, are a growing mattress trend. These bases require mattresses designed to accommodate them. If you like to sit up and read while your partner sleeps, look into connecting two twin mattresses with adjustable bases. Some couples solve their mattress disagreements with a Sleep Number bed, which allows each partner to dial in the firmness they prefer. If you're easily awakened when your partner stirs, look for a mattress that has motion isolation, meaning when your partner stirs, your side of the mattress stays still. If you run hot, look for mattresses with air flow, gel, or other cooling features.

How big? Queen-size bed sets are by far the most popular in

America at over 40 percent of all mattress sales, for good reason; queen beds fit two average-sized adults comfortably. Visually, they look most pleasing in primary bedrooms.

Medical perspective. "A bad mattress won't damage your back, but it can cause you to have a sore back in the morning and cause poor sleep," said Dr. Stephane Lavoie, a Central Florida spinal surgeon. "When dealing with lower back pain that's the result of an arthritic condition, having more support can offer relief." (Apparently, based on the statistics, 80 percent of you know what I'm talking about.) A medium-firm mattress appears to provide the best combination of comfort and support compared to mattresses that are too soft or too hard. That said, while most buyers want a "medium-firm" mattress, no industry standard exists for measuring firmness. Experts define proper "support" as when your mattress keeps your spine aligned, and in a neutral position, minimizing any curves, as if you were standing up with good posture.

In short, a new or different mattress can bring relief to those who wake up with stiff backs. Conversely, sleeping on an old mattress, or one that isn't a good fit, can lead to or increase morning back stiffness. But no mattress will cause or cure a back problem.

What's inside? Innerspring mattresses are most popular, but two of five customers choose memory foam or a hybrid. One third of customers want a pillowtop, a mattress plus a comfort layer. When considering a mattress that incorporates foam, look for high foam density, north of 1.8 pound. The greater the density, the longer the mattress will last.

Read the fine print. Don't put too much stock in the number of years on a mattress warranty. Most warranties have huge loopholes and out clauses. Do, however, look closely at the return policy. Find out if the seller will refund or exchange the mattress if you're unhappy. Some retailers let you try and return a mattress after a short period of time if you're not satisfied. The returns may or may not be free. Some will take the mattress back only if you buy another mattress. Others will charge a restocking fee.

Caring for Your Mattress

To extend the life of your mattress and help it wear evenly, turn or rotate it once a year. If your mattress is the same on both sides, flip it. If it has a pillowtop, or is a one-sided mattress, you can't turn it over, but you can rotate it and put the head at the foot. Always use a mattress protector, a layer between your fitted sheet and the mattress, which will not only protect the mattress but will also add a buffering layer of insulation.

Summary: Choosing Your Mattress

- The best way to know if you like a mattress is to sleep on it.

- Any new mattress is better than an old one. Replace yours every seven to ten years.

- Hotel mattresses are made of tougher stuff and may be worth investigating.

- You're not dreaming. A bad mattress can exacerbate a back condition, and a good one can provide relief. But no mattress will cause or cure a back problem.

- Know the return policy.

CHAPTER 22

Don't Short Your Sheets

When Westin Hotels came out with the Heavenly Bed in 1999, they performed a huge public service. The multi-layered all-white and crisp Heavenly Bed was a dream compared to what weary travelers were used to turning down. Thankfully, other hotels caught on.

While this was a giant step forward for the hotel industry, don't be fooled. The Heavenly Bed should be the low bar for homes. Folks, these beds are made with industrial-strength sheets designed to put up with laundering temperatures hotter than the surface of the sun and detergents stronger than jet fuel.

You deserve finer.

If the Heavenly Bed feels like a step up from your bedding at home, I ask you, where are your standards? Excellent sheets are not a luxury. They are a necessity. Remember: *the closer something is to your body, the better it should be.*

MARNI MANTRA:

The closer something is to your body, the better it should be.

A former schoolteacher, Missy Tannen, of Chatham, New Jersey, got into the bed-linen business after she and her husband remodeled their primary bedroom. She went in search of the ideal linens to finish the room. She couldn't find what she wanted, so her husband said, "Why don't you make them?"

Off she went. In January 2014, she launched Boll & Branch, which today is one of the world's largest makers of luxury sheets, with annual sales of over $100 million.

I've talked to Missy many times over the years and used her company's products. What I like about her bed linens is that she created them for herself. Her feminine sensibility is apparent in the meticulous attention to detail, like the choice of edging.

While other sheets in addition to hers meet all the criteria I'm about to share with you, Tannen taught me what to look for and what not to settle for. You want your sheets to check all the boxes.

Buying bed linens right, by knowing what to look for, means you won't end up with five sets of sheets in your linen closet that you can't stand because they scratch, pill, don't fit the mattress, or don't breathe. Not knowing what to look for in bed linens, like other household basics, results in a frustrating trial-and-error cycle and overstuffed linen closets.

Picking the Perfect Sheet

"We all use bed linens every single day," Tannen said. "So why do so many people put up with sheets they don't love?"

"Because," I said, "they don't know what to look for."

Well, now you do. So we can find soft sheets that breathe and get better, not worse, with age. Tannen helped me create a checklist.

- **Know what you like.** Fine sheets are either crisp (percale) or soft (sateen). Both can be dreamy depending on the quality of cotton. The difference is weave. In percale sheets, the cross thread goes over one thread and under one thread, creating a tight weave and a crisp feel. The sheets make little peaks, so air circulates underneath. Both sides of a percale sheet look the same. In sateen sheets, one thread crosses over four threads and under one, which makes a looser, softer fabric that drapes softly. It has a right side, and a back side. A good sateen is soft and breathes.

- **Examine the cotton quality.** Read the label closely. You want 100 percent (not 95 percent or 97 percent) combed, organic cotton. Yes, I know, 100-percent cotton wrinkles, whereas permanent press sheets (where the fabric is treated with a chemical, often resin, to make it wrinkle-resistant) are wrinkle free. But if you want sheets that breathe and don't smother, you must adopt a zero-synthetic policy. Combed cotton means short cotton fibers have been combed out leaving only long cotton fibers, which resist pilling. With un-combed cotton sheets, short fibers pop out, twist, matt, and pill like a cheap sweater. You see this happen on lower-quality cotton T-shirts. Certified organic means makers did not use genetically modified seeds or any chemicals during the manufacturing process.

- **Watch for cheap tricks.** Sheet makers often coat sheets with waxy chemicals that give them a shiny look and silky feel. These additives gloss over the roughness of lower-quality fabrics, which eventually pokes through. After a few washings, the coating is stripped away, leaving behind raw disappointment. They also cut corners, literally. That is, they make top sheets just a little shorter, or narrower, and skimp on fitted sheets so they don't quite fit over, say, a fifteen-inch pillowtop mattress. Check the thickness of your mattress and compare dimension. You want generous.

- **Read between the threads.** Thread count is a poor measure of quality because it can be manipulated. While it's true that a higher thread count (i.e., more threads per inch) equals a finer sheet, one thread can be made of one, two, or three plies of cotton fiber twisted together. Some makers inflate their thread count by counting plies, not threads. Thus, they count one three-ply thread as three threads and triple their thread count, claiming a 450-thread count, when it's really 150. Great sheets have a single-ply thread count of 300 to 400. Higher than that is not likely possible, unless you count plies.

- **Note the finer details.** Smaller stitches and well-appointed trims on top sheets and pillowcase edges separate ordinary bed linens from the stuff of gods. Nice finishing details not only suggest higher quality but can also underscore your style, whether formal, vintage, preppy, contemporary, or classic.

- **Test-drive the pillowcase.** Before investing in a full set of sheets, buy just the pillowcases. Wash and use them to see how you like the fabric feel before you invest in a full set.

- **Good sheets are expensive.** A good set of sheets can cost one-hundred to two-hundred dollars or more. That may seem like a lot but not when you consider that you crawl between them at night and spend one-third of your life next to them. Sheets are one of the few items you can invest in that you can appreciate from head to toe.

- **All you need.** When you buy sheets right, all you need are two sets. One on the bed, and one to use to change the bed. No more clogging up your linen closet with subpar sheets.

Caring for Your Sheets

Once you've found (and paid for) those dreamy sheets that embrace you like an angel's wings, make sure they last. "Great sheets should not get rougher or fall apart after many washings," said Tannen, and they won't if you start with the right sheets and wash them correctly.

Proper care can also help them maintain their brightness. To get the scoop on how to get keep my white sheets white, I turned to Wayne Edelman, of Meurice Garment Care, a high-end cleaner based in New York, where he is affectionately known as the stainmaster. Edelman grew up in the family cleaning business, which his father started in 1961, the year the younger Edelman was born. The company is now a large luxury cleaning service with a high-end clientele that includes fashion houses, museums, private collectors, and couture garments for celebrities. "We clean priceless collections," Edelman said, recalling the day Princess Di's gowns arrived in an armored car.

I soon realized this man's laundry advice could change my life, and it has. Here's what he advises when cleaning and caring for household linens:

- **Be realistic.** "Many people don't understand that white is a color," he said. "They think it's the absence of color, and that all fabrics are white at their core. But white textiles are dyed white and fade like any other color." However, sometimes soil and residue are the reason they've lost their luster, in which case proper laundering can help.

- **First off, avoid softeners.** Adding fabric softener or using dryer sheets coats sheets and towels, reducing their absorbency and breathability. In short, it makes them feel icky. Sheets and towels should never feel slippery, slick, or waxy.

- **Avoid chlorine bleach.** It can dull colors and break down fabrics. "Save the chlorine bleach for your fountains and pools," he said. "The best way to brighten and restore dingy or stained white household linens is to soak them in warm water, laundry detergent, and a sodium-based bleach like OxiClean overnight."

- **Bet on the laundry trifecta:** time, temperature, and concentration. The duration of the wash cycle matters. A longer wash will remove more soil than a short one. Although heat can shrink some material, don't be afraid of warm water. It will keep whites whiter and increase the chances of stain removal. And don't skimp on the soap, but don't go overboard either, or garments can get sticky. In summary, go for long wash cycles, warm water, plenty of detergent, and a sodium-based bleach.

- **Wash bedding weekly or a least every two weeks.** Frequent washing is especially important if you have allergies. Dust mites love to nest in beds. Keep them out by wrapping pillows and mattresses in dust-mite-proof pillow covers. Wash sheets and blankets in water that's at least 130 degrees Fahrenheit. Wash pillows, mattress pads and comforters often as well.

- **Wash towels separately.** Towel lint can stick to sheets in the dryer, so sheets come out coated with lint balls. Plus, towels are rough and can "beat up" sheets in the washer and dryer.

- **Shake 'em up.** A few brisk shakes of the sheets between wash and dry cycles will reduce wrinkles. If you put a crumpled ball of wet sheets right into the dryer, the creases bake in.

- **Air dry when you can.** "Dryers are hard on clothes," Edelman said. "Of course, you have to put towels and blankets in the dryer, and I dry sheets there, too. Not everyone can string up a clothesline. But I do hang or lay flat smaller items to dry, or remove them from the dryer when they are not quite dry. The last bit of drying is when shrinkage happens."

- **Don't overdry.** When you machine dry, use low heat, and remove sheets from the dryer when they're still warm.

- **Don't steam-iron cottons and linens.** "Iron cottons and linens when they're damp," he said. "If the item you want to iron is dry, sprinkle or spritz it with water and iron at the recommended temperature. Don't steam iron. What gives cotton and linen that crisp finish is pulling the water out of the damp fabric with a hot dry iron. "Steam ironing forces water in and makes the fabric limp."

- **Hot tip.** Edelman believes all sheets should be pressed. (I'm working on it.) "That best emulates a luxe hotel," he said. A shortcut to get that pressed look is to iron only the top twelve inches of the sheet, which you see when it's turned back, and the pillowcases. The rest stays undercover.

Summary: Choosing Your Sheets

- Know whether you prefer percale (crisp) or sateen (soft) sheets.

- Look for 100-percent combed organic cotton.

- Look for a *single-ply* thread count of 300 to 400.

- Look for generous dimensions. Be sure the contour sheet will fit your mattress thickness.

- Note the details, such as fine stitching.

- Test a set of pillowcases before you commit.

Change Your Bedding with the Season

In Florida, where I live, August nights are hotter than stars. They make fans swirl like skirts at a square dance, and bed covers fly off like candy wrappers on Halloween. August nights are so hot, they make us sleep like starfish. The dogs leave their plush beds to sprawl on cool tile. I've been tempted to join them, but instead I went in search of other cool ways to get through summer nights.

Yes, I know we can crank up the air conditioning, but let's not waste the energy. Let's change the bedding. Wherever you live, your bed in August should not be dressed the same as it is in January, with a thick down comforter, dark wool blankets, and heavy sheets. If it is, you need to change more than your thermostat.

When building your bed in summer, think winter in reverse. In cooler months, most of us want thick bedding to keep the warm in and the cold out; in summer, we want the warm out and the cool in. Here are four ways to make a cool bed in hot weather. Do this in reverse for cold weather:

1. **Put away the duvet.** The first step to a cooler bed is to store the heavy down duvet or comforter in the armoire or blanket chest until fall. Replace it with an all-cotton or linen quilt or coverlet.

2. **Cool it on color.** Dark colors not only look hot, they are hotter because they absorb more heat. Remove bedding in dark colors like rust, navy, burgundy, charcoal and brown, and replace it with a lighter palette of breezy pastels and white.

3. **Change the sheets.** While storing your heavy comforter and dark blankets, put away other dense bedding like flannel or heavier sheets. In summer, you want sheets that are light, breathable, and absorbent. The breathe is in the weave. Linen sheets offer a cooler

option. Derived from the flax plant, linen is the most breathable sheet fabric, so it lends itself to a cooler sleep. However, some find that linen feels too rough, as it is not as smooth as cotton (though it does soften with age and washing).

4. **The coolest sleeping cotton sheets are percale.** Some may prefer sateen in colder months. Being a stiffer, crisper fabric, percale keeps you cooler because it doesn't settle over you but rather makes little tents, which allow more air to circulate.

5. **As for polyester sheets, avoid them.** You never hear anyone say, "I love my polyester sheets."

6. **Revisit your mattress pad.** These can have a big effect on body temperature when you sleep. Ones made of memory foam, for instance, can sleep hot. However, cooling mattress pads that allow more air to circulate are available.

7. **Use lighter layers.** Layering is not just for looks, it's for function. Because many summer sleepers want to feel the weight of a cover but not the heat, the solution lies in light, breathable layers. Combine a light top sheet, a light blanket, and a cotton or linen quilt or coverlet until you find the right combination. Start with one or two layers and have a third at the foot of the bed ready to pull up if you cool down.

CHAPTER 23

When Picking a Pillow, Use Your Head

You snuggle with them. You sleep with them. You hold them close. Some of you won't leave home without them. No, I'm not talking about your pet. I'm talking about your pillow— that unsung household hero that most of us spend more face time with than any other object, save for, sadly, our phones.

That said, and we can keep this between us, when was the last time you replaced yours? Or washed it? I see the color in your cheeks.

What good is a dreamy new mattress and sheet set if your pillow is a nasty, drool-stained, dust-filled lump that is half its original size?

"When we find that favorite pillow, we act as if it should last for decades," said Mary Helen Rogers, spokeswoman for the Better Sleep Council. "But the materials in pillows, like any soft product, wear over time."

Her council's researchers and other experts suggest that if you use a pillow nightly, its lifespan is about three years. Besides age, another clue that your pillow needs replacing is when it looks lumpy and uneven. When you replace your pillow, don't, that is, *do not*, put the old biohazard in the linen closet. Toss it!

If you wake up with allergy symptoms like itchy, watery eyes, a stuffy nose, or fits of sneezing, your old pillow could the problem. Over time, pillows, like mattresses, collect dust mites and other allergens. Wash your pillow (see care instructions) and see if the problem resolves. You could also be allergic to the down-feather fill.

Like mattresses, pillows are personal. What I love, you may not. But we can agree that sleeping on the wrong pillow can be a pain in the neck. So here are some pillow pointers to sleep on:

- **Run pillow check.** To find out if your pillows are ripe for replacement, look at them. If they're stained or discolored, wash or replace them. Smell them. If a pillow smells musty, dusty, and old, it is. Fold it in half. If it stays folded when you let go, it's dead. Pillows should look clean, smell fresh, and rebound.

- **Find your fill.** For comfort, softness, air circulation and durability, down-feather is your fill. Good quality down and feather will outlast just about any pillow fill material in the market. Down, the fluffy stuff under bird feathers, adds loft and softness, while feathers add structure and support. If you're allergic to down, opt for a good down alternative. Less expensive and also popular are polyester-fill pillows, which feel firmer than down. Bamboo pillows, popular for their softness and for being made from material that is highly sustainable and that replenishes itself quickly, come in varying degrees of firmness. Latex offers even more firmness, though it's not for those who like to fluff their pillow at night. Foam provides a firmer feel, which some like, but they can get warm and break down faster. Memory-foam pillows adjust to your shape as you move, and newer versions offer temperature control.

- **Understand fill power.** Like thread count in sheets, fill power in pillows offers a way to rate quality in synthetic or natural down pillow. The higher the number, the better the pillow. Aim for fill-power of 600 or higher.
- **Keep them covered.** Add a layer between the pillow and the pillowcase by inserting a pillow protector. You want these to be 100-percent cotton and zippered. Pillow protectors help keep dust, moisture, and stains away from the pillow and lengthen its life.

Caring for Your Pillows

Wash your pillows twice a year. Check your pillow's care instructions. Most can be machine washed and dried. Use a tiny amount of detergent, and add a second rinse cycle to get all the soap out. You may also need to run bed pillows through the dryer more than once to get the middle dry. Adding a tennis ball or two to the dry cycle can help fluff pillows back up.

Summary: Choosing Pillows

- Replace pillows used nightly every three years.

- Fill is personal, but most prefer down-feather or, if allergic, a polyester-down alternative.

- Look for a fill-power of 600 or higher.

- Put a pillow protector between the pillow and the pillowcase.

CHAPTER 24

Curing Closet Chaos

Before I leave the bedroom, let me say a word about your clothes closet. Actually, several words: purge, organize, and get new hangers.

If your rightsizing involves moving to a new home, your closet may not be your first priority. Don't worry about putting everything away in just the right place on moving day. Just come close and keep moving. Moving day involves making thousands of game-time decisions about where and how stuff will go in the new home. You have to move fast, which is how the sewing basket ends up in the dog-kibble bin, because if you aim for perfection, you could spend the whole day on the silverware drawer.

But *eventually*, you need to revisit and reorganize storage areas, starting with your closets.

Hanger Management

An organized, clutter-free closet guarantees you will begin and end your days with at least some part of your life under control. Folks, if you don't want to live with a tangled hanger jungle looming over a knee-deep shoe pile with a janky-smelling laundry basket shoved in the corner, follow the ten steps below.

- **Take everything out.** *Ooof!* I know. It's ugly and a hassle. But trust me. As with any major organizing project, the situation looks worse before it looks better.

- **Shop your clothes.** With all your clothes out of the closet, choose to keep, rather than choose to let go. In other words, rather than rifle through your clothes looking for what to get rid of, work in reverse. Hold up every item and ask yourself, *Would I buy this again for my life now?* If you are retired, you can probably get rid of your business wardrobe, or much of it. If it is stained, torn, missing a button, doesn't fit, or you never wear it, get rid of it. I don't care how much it cost.

- **Eliminate duplicates.** As you cull the pile, don't just weed out the old, stained, worn, ill-fitting, and unflattering. Look for redundancy. If you have six pairs of black pants, maybe you only need two or three. Let the rest go.

- **Have a trial separation pile.** When waffling over a garment, rather than err on the side of keeping it, put it in a "trial separation" box. Revisit these items in a few months to make a final call. This way you don't lose momentum or cling too much.

- **Start with a clean slate.** Because it's likely to be a while before your closet is empty again, wipe down all the shelves, and sweep or vacuum the floor.

- **Configure your closet.** Your closet should accommodate your clothes. Don't try to make your clothes fit the current configuration of your closet. Design the space to fit your edited wardrobe by category. Decide what you want to hang, fold, or roll. In general, fold and stack sweaters and sweat-shirts. Hang dresses, shirts, slacks, and skirts. Measure for long-hang versus short-hang items. File-fold thinner items upright in drawers. That is, arrange them so the thin edges are up, like slices in a loaf of bread, so you can see the edge of each garment. Make the structural changes—add shelving, another hanging rod, drawers, bins, or racks for shoes, belts, ties, or scarves—to accommodate your clothes. Factor in your height. My closet's prior owner was at least six inches taller than I am. I had been stretching and cursing trying to reach high shelves. Why? This was my closet. I took the rods and shelves down a few pegs to accommodate my shorter clothes and height. *Duh.*

- **Use the whole wall.** No matter your stature, you can still make use of some of the unreachable feet of space near the ceiling. Put in a high shelf to store lesser-used items, such as suitcases, or off-season sweaters. Keep a stepstool handy, so these items are always in reach.

- **Unify your hangers.** Trade out your mismatched plastic hangers for slim, velvet, non-slip hangers. This will change your life. Having uniform matching hangers will instantly usher in order and literally make a measurable difference. One pack of fifty slim, non-slip hangers costs around twenty-four dollars, about fifty cents each. These hangers are half the width of typical plastic hangers. (You're not using wire hangers, right? Good. Just making sure. Try returning them to your cleaners to recycle if they will accept them. (Not all do.) A stack of twelve slim velvet hangers measures two inches; a stack of twelve plastic dress hangers measures four inches. So for every twelve garments on velvet non-slip hangers, you gain two inches of rod space. You want more hanging space, so your clothes aren't crammed? You just got it.

- **Replace with care.** Resist the temptation to put your clothes back as they were before. Think about what wasn't working—stacks were too deep, belts were tangled—and eliminate pain points. Organize by type of clothing, sleeve length, and then color.

- **Maintain the order.** To keep your rightsized wardrobe under control, purge your clothes seasonally, at the end of summer and the end of winter. Practice the one-in, one-out rule. (If you get a new pair of jeans, get rid of a pair.) Ignore the one-year rule. Whoever said you should get rid of any garment you haven't worn in a year has never spent $100 on a piece of clothing, been pregnant, skipped the holiday party, or lived through the pandemic. If it still fits, is in good condition, you like it and would wear it again, *keep* it. Recency of use should not be your criteria.

THE BATHROOM

Refresh, Rejuvenate, Relax

What soap is to the body, laughter is to the soul.
—Victor Borge, Danish comedian

The smallest, most personal room in the house, bathrooms often fall short of their full potential because many of us treat them as a pit stop. We zoom in and zoom out.

But what if this transitional place were more like a sanctuary and less like a locker room?

In your rightsized life, the room where you start and end every day should be a refuge, a place where thoughtful consideration goes into everything that touches your senses.

We'll start with the basics, getting the right towels and soap, and then we'll end with ways to make your bathroom feel like a spa.

CHAPTER 25

The Quest for the Perfect Bath Towel

Folks, I've been watching you. And you're doing it all wrong. I've seen you in the towel aisle, picking towels based on feel, right? You go for plush. The softer and thicker, the better.

Well, you're being gamed by one of the oldest tricks in the industry. Towel makers coat their product with sizing chemicals exactly so people say, "Ooh, that feels soft!" and dump four sets in their carts.

Hold up. That towel you buy in the store is not the towel you end up with.

That sizing that feels so silky soft actually blocks fibers from absorbing, so towels wind up pushing water around on your skin like a squeegee. What you want are towels that drink water like camels in the desert. When that soft sizing washes out—which is a good thing—you're left with a towel that feels nothing like what you bought. You feel betrayed.

Towels are like people: you don't really know them until you've lived with them.

"A great towel is soft, durable, and absorbent," said Missy Tannen, founder of Boll & Branch, who, after she spent months traveling the world and learning how to find the best cotton for sheets, turned her attention to cotton for towels.

"On my search, I found soft towels that wouldn't last, absorbent towels that weren't soft, and towels so thick they wouldn't dry between uses so they got that mildew smell," she said.

She kept looking for the three-in-one towel trifecta: soft, thirsty, and just the right weight. Ultimately, she found it. Then she shared what we all should look for when picking that perfect towel. Hint: it's not that first feel.

- **Check the cotton.** You want 100-percent, high-grade cotton with a long staple. A cotton staple refers to the length of the natural fiber. Better cotton, such as Egyptian cotton, has a longer staple. Longer fibers make cotton more durable.

- **Take in the side show.** Look at the towel from the side to see how high the pile is, or the loop of the cotton. Higher means softer. Inferior towels tend to skimp on pile height.

- **Look for a twist.** The loop should also have a twist in it. That twist is what makes a towel thirsty. You want towels to suck up water like a football team at summer training camp.

- **Get a happy medium.** Too-thin towels feel skimpy, too thick won't dry overnight. Plus, try drying the inside of your ear with a bulky towel. You can't. Look for midweight.

- **Mind the details.** You want small stitches along the finished edges, a sign of better craftsmanship.
- **Avoid color.** I like white towels. They have nothing to hide, don't fade, and, if you wash your facecloth three times more often than your hand towel, the set will still match. Plus, asking your towels to add color to your bathroom is like asking your toilet paper to be a decorative accessory. These are service items. Add color with artwork.
- **Skip the embellishments.** Appliqués of ribbon or flower bouquets or other decorative motifs on towels can look cheesy and get even worse after washings. Keep towels simple, clean, and beautiful.
- **Take one for a test drive.** Before you commit to a full set, buy a hand towel. Wash it a few times, use it, and see how it looks, feels, functions, and holds up.

Caring for Your Towels

Wash towels before you use them. Launder them separately from other clothes. To keep them white, use a sodium-based (not chlorine) bleach, and wash in warm water. Never use softeners. Dry on medium heat and don't overdry.

Summary: Choosing Your Bath Towels

- Look for 100-percent, high-grade cotton, such as Egyptian cotton, with a long staple.

- Look for loops with a twist and a mid-weight pile.

- Avoid embellishments and colors. Stick with white.

CHAPTER 26

Sophisticated Suds

I didn't always appreciate the difference between commercial soaps and their upscale cousins. Growing up, I just used whatever Mom put in the bathroom. No one worked up much of a lather over whether that was Dial, Zest, Jergens, Dove, Palmolive, or Irish Spring. ("Clean as a Whistle!")

That changed when I took my first trip to France as an adult. I became so enamored of French soap that I brought home a dozen bars. These soaps had that *je ne sais quoi* (only now I do know) that made them so much better than the stuff from American grocery stores. Was it the heavy, solid feel of the bar in my hand, the smooth refined texture, the rich creamy lather, the natural but not overpowering natural scents?

Yes.

Unlike those harsher-scented bars that smell like the exhaust from a dryer vent, these French soaps would lift me on a little-scented cloud and transport me to a citrus grove, a flower garden in spring, or a wooded glen.

Though I knew this experience existed, I considered it a splurge, a treat on special occasions or vacations. Until one day, when I again got my hands on a great bar of soap, I asked myself, *Why not use the good stuff every day?*

Soap Science

As luxuries go, buying fine soap is a pretty small extravagance. As long as you are now dedicated to living well, here's what you should know and look for in a soap.

- **Know your soap basics.** Soaps are a combination of fat (animal or vegetable) and alkaline (or lye). When mixed, a chemical reaction occurs called *saponification*—a fancy way to say it turns into a substance that binds to grime and removes it. When fat and alkaline combine, they form crystals, which are rough. Soap makers refine the crystals using a variety of methods including cold pressing and machine milling. Here's the secret: the more milling, the finer the soap.

- **Look for triple milled.** The French invented the milling process in the eighteenth century and have perfected it. The process involves shredding cold-processed soap and then running it through three or more rollers to press it. Hence the name French milled or triple milled. This makes soap harder, so a bar lasts much longer than commercial soaps. It also makes the lather finer and richer, so soap feels creamier and smoother on the skin. The bubbles in the suds are actually smaller. Unlike single-milled soap bars, which tend to fall apart when half used, triple-milled soap is stable to the end.

> For a premium bar of soap, expect to pay at least twice what you pay for a commercial soap.

- **Don't fall for false fragrance.** When consumers buy specialty soap, the first thing they often do is to smell it, so soap makers often amp up the scent with manufactured fragrances. But a soap's scent shouldn't overwhelm. Many natural ingredients, like almond, oat, and coconut, have little to no scent. If you smell something "coconut-scented" that reminds you of suntan oil, you can bet it's not natural. Natural scents come from essential oils like citrus, cedar, lavender, lemongrass, and peppermint. Purists who don't want a soap's scent to compete with their cologne or perfume can choose unscented bars.

- **Pay the price.** For a premium bar of soap, expect to pay at least twice what you pay for a commercial soap. I buy French-milled soap—lemon-verbena, lavender, and green tea—for $3.49 a bar at Trader Joe's. If you think that's just money down the drain, try it. You'll adjust.

Summary: Choosing Soap

- Get triple milled.
- Don't fall for false scents.

Seven Ways to Spa-tify Your Bath

Though we can't always relax in a dreamy spa when we'd like to, we can create our own pretty easily right in our own home. Here are seven ways to spa-tify your bathroom:

1. **Declutter.** Clutter and calm cannot coexist. Clear counters in the bathroom help create a tranquil feel. Everything on your bathroom counters should be both beautiful and useful.

2. **Cut the commercials.** To eliminate visual noise, hide labels, cover tissue boxes, put liquid soaps and lotions in attractive pump dispensers, and fill elegant jars with cotton balls and Q-Tips. If it isn't pretty, make it pretty, or don't set it out.

3. **Organize.** Edit your bathroom drawers and cabinets. Toss any products you don't use. Once you've pared down, get drawer organizers. Bath products have a way of sprawling. Corral shower products into a handsome, well-made caddy. Place bath essentials on a chic tray by the tub. Maximize tall storage under the sink with stackable wire baskets. Leave room for a small waste bin and keep it out of sight.

4. **Make it gleam.** Your bathroom should look, smell, and feel like the most hygienic room in the house. Make every surface—from mirrors and showers to faucets and toilet bowls—gleam. To create a Zen vibe, keep patterns to a minimum and color palettes light.

5. **Add light control.** Because sometimes you want good light (when applying make-up or shaving), and other

times soft light, when winding down before bed, install dimmers. This will give you instant mood control at the touch of a button.

6. **Splurge on little luxuries.** Add a sumptuous bathmat and a plush terry robe. Because you really don't want to use yesterday's washcloth, buy a dozen, and keep them nearby in a neat stack or roll them in a pretty basket.

7. **Appeal to your "scentses."** Spas are filled with soothing scents, usually fragrances like eucalyptus, lavender, and citrus. Find a scent you love and purchase candles and soaps in that scent.

Then grab that cushy robe, draw a steamy bath, light a scented candle, pour a chilled beverage, and close the door, leaving the noisy world outside.

THE LIVING AREA

Where Life Happens

*Things are only worth
what you make them worth.*
—Moliere

I f the kitchen is the most popular room in the house, our living areas are the most public. It's where we hang out and entertain friends. As a result, it's the room most people decorate first and want to look good.

I've heard many designers say, if you can only splurge on one item in your home, make it a great rug. Others, like interior designer Ken Olsen, say, "I tell my clients to spend their money on the places where they put their bodies the most, like your mattress and the sofa you sit on daily."

I think both are right. But what makes a great rug great, and how do you know a high-quality sofa? Let's find out.

CHAPTER 27

Oriental Rugs: Removing the Mystery, Finding the Value

When putting together the room where we live, most interior designers will recommend starting from the ground up, with a great rug. They will also say that rugs make a home.

Indeed, a well-placed Oriental rug, that is, one hand-knotted from Asia, can be the soul of a room. Of course, unless you have the rug, investing in the rug first is fantasyland. In the real world, rugs come last: "That's a beautiful rug, honey, but what are we going to sleep on?" However, if you're serious about filling your home with quality and not with second-rate furnishings, this is one place to pause, learn, and possibly splurge.

In my experience, choosing a main area rug is the single most difficult home design decision one can make. That's because so many factors need to click: style, material, pattern, scale, quality, motif, size, color, and wiliest of all, value for the price. How do you know if the seller—and carpet dealers are notorious for this—is pulling the carpet wool over your eyes?

I get that some rugs, like some wines, are very valuable, and others are not. What I wanted to know was how to tell the difference. Determined to get to the bottom of this mystery and also to outfit my own home with rugs that will last a lifetime, I turned to two experts. Hakan Zor is a fifth-generation Turkish carpet merchant with clients throughout the United States.

Robert Mann, owner of Robert Mann Rugs, in Denver, Colorado, is one of the foremost rug authorities in the country. Mann has worked in the rug industry for forty-five years. He has made, repaired, sold, cleaned, and appraised rugs. Today, he runs a large rug-cleaning and repair facility.

"The industry is not transparent," Mann said, adding that years ago, the occasional unscrupulous rug merchant gave the industry a bad name. "Fortunately, today the Internet can vet a lot of lies."

Since getting educated, I have purchased several Oriental rugs, which I would not part with. I appreciate owning these beautifully handcrafted pieces that are part of a dwindling art form that dates to the fifth century BC.

I've learned that fine handmade rugs are pieces of art. Better ones, Zor has taught me, will have intricate patterns, numerous colors, and well-executed (not jagged) lines. They will be made of all-natural handspun fibers, such as wool or silk. (If you comb your hand over the rug's surface, you won't come up with fuzz.)

Clearly, I got bitten by the rug bug.

Yet, I still remember waking up the morning after I invested in my first Oriental rug, a ten-by-fourteen that I put in my family room, thinking I'd made a terrible mistake. I called my friend Beverly Hills designer Christopher Grubb, whom you met in Chapter 9, and who is no stranger to high-end furnishings. I sent him photos of my great room before and after the new rug, a Haji Jalili style woven probably a couple of decades earlier in India. I tell him I am on the verge of an acute case of buyer's remorse.

"Be honest," I say.

"Do you have to ask?" says Grubb.

"Yes!"

"The carpet is fantastic in your room, better than fantastic. It brings the room to life. And the scale is perfect."

"But couldn't we have achieved that for a lot less?"

After a long pause, he delivers the news I did not want to hear: "Not after you know what a good rug looks like, and you can tell this is a very good rug. You're an expert now. You appreciate the value. You saw the process involved in making rugs like this and can't look at rugs the same way again."

Then he added, "You buy certain things in life not because you're going to make a profit but because you are filling a desire. At some point you need to say, we've got this one life, and you go for it."

If you are going to go down the path of buying fine collectibles—and I am not recommending it—first, get educated. Train your eye. Then find an expert you trust to advise you, someone with many years' experience and a good reputation. Finally, though items *may* hold their value, don't do it for money. Do it for love.

"You don't buy an Oriental rug as an investment," Mann said. "You do it to make yourself happy. That's the only logical reason. The value comes from your appreciation and enjoyment of it."

How to Judge a Rug

While we can't all become rug aficionados like Mann and Zor, here's what we can consider when assessing an area rug for our home:

- **Know the difference between hand-knotted and machine-made.** Most rugs in stores today are machine-made, and that's fine if you like how they look and don't overpay. But finer rugs are hand-knotted. You can tell by looking at the back. If the rug has a rubber-like backing, it is machine-made. Handmade carpets do not have a backing, so you can see the hand-tied knot work. If the fringe on the end is stitched on, the rug is not handmade.

- **Natural fibers.** Most mass-produced rugs are made of machine-spun fibers, which are often synthetic. Better rugs are made of 100 handspun natural fibers such as wool, cotton, and silk. (Silk rugs are very expensive and not anything you'd want anyone to put their feet on.)

- **Natural versus synthetic dyes.** The colors in mass-produced rugs typically come from chemical dyes, while finer rugs have fibers colored with natural or vegetal dyes, from plants, insect, or animal sources. Though all colors fade over time, chemical colors fade faster. When buying a high-end rug, sniff it. If it smells like petroleum, the maker probably used synthetic materials or dyes. All-natural rugs do not smell like chemicals.

- **Pattern.** In general, the more colors in a handmade rug, and the more intricate its pattern, the greater its value.

- **Knot count.** The more knots a rug has per inch, the finer the rug, the more time it took to weave, and the higher the value. Thus, a silk rug at 1,200 knots per inch will have a much higher value than a wool rug with 360 knots per square inch.

To find out the knots per inch (kpi), put a ruler on the backside of a hand-knotted rug and count the number of stitches per inch each way. If you get ten knots up and ten across, the rug has 100 (kpi), and 14,400 per square foot (100 x 144 square inches).

- **Labor.** In one day, the average weaver working at a loom might tie 6,000 knots, Mann said. On a nine-by-twelve-foot rug, three weavers working side by side (three feet per weaver), could collectively tie 18,000 knots in a day. A nine-foot-wide rug with 100 kpi would have 129,600 knots for every foot-length of rug and would take three weavers seven days to weave. If they worked five days a week, it would take them about four months to finish a twelve-foot rug. That doesn't include the time it takes to harvest, spin, and dye the wool.

See what I mean about appreciating this dying art? To verify that illegal child labor wasn't involved in the making of a rug you're interested in, ask the rug merchant whether the rug was made using fair and ethical practices. Fortunately, thanks to better oversight and trade restrictions, the illegal practice of using children to weave rugs is also fading away.

- **Cost per square foot.** That is how the industry calculates cost, and you should, too. Say a producer's cost, for labor, materials and transportation to ship rugs to a US warehouse, comes out to fifteen dollars a square foot. He will generally sell rugs to a buyer for twice that, or thirty dollars. That rug buyer then tags the item for retail sale at three times that, or ninety dollars a square foot, but he'd be happy to get sixty dollars. Keep this supply chain in mind when negotiating. Negotiating with rug dealers is part of the process and something they expect.

- **Fact-check.** Go into a store and ask questions. What type of rug is this? Where was it made? What's it made of? (Look for 100 percent wool on cotton.) How many knots per inch? Take notes and pictures. When you find out it's, say, a 16/18 Pakistan, search Google images to find out what it should cost.

- **Thinness.** Many consumers incorrectly believe that the plusher the rug, the better, when the opposite is true. Pile length relates to the tightness of knots. The tighter the knot, or the more knots per square inch, the shorter the pile; the bigger the knot, the higher the pile. "In the Middle East there's a saying. You can tell how rich a person is by how thin their rugs are," Mann said.

- **Try before you buy.** Most rug sellers know you will want to see the rug in your home before you buy it and will encourage you to take a rug you're considering, or even several, home for a test drive. Accept this offer. Some may want a refundable deposit while you try rugs out.

Caring for Your Rugs

You probably don't want to know what's lurking in your area rugs. Many are designed to hide your dirt, dust, and dander, and they do a brilliant job. But ignoring reality only works for so long. I have dogs, which means I know the number of my rug cleaner by heart. When you need your rugs cleaned, you have two options: steam clean in your home or, for a more thorough job, send them out to a rug-washing plant. If an area rug is only lightly soiled, having it steam cleaned in your home may be all you need to do to refresh it. In-home steam cleaning typically costs about $1 a square foot.

However, if the rug has badly soiled traffic areas or pet or food stains that have soaked in, you're better off sending it out for a professional soak. If the rug is a high-value rug, professional cleaning is a worthy investment that will help the rug last. Off-site rug washing typically runs $4 to $5 a square foot. When looking online for an offsite rug washing facility, the key is to search "rug washing," not "rug cleaning." Cleaning implies steam cleaning in the home. Check the company's website for photos or videos, and make sure the business is legit and established.

The Turkish Bath for Rugs

I was skeptical about this off-site washing process. How did I know this wasn't just a couple of guys in their driveway washing rugs with a garden hose? I agreed to send my rugs out as long as I could visit the plant to see it for myself.

At First Impressions in Winter Garden, Florida, owner Kurt Gilbertson gave me a tour.

At his plant, rugs first stop at the dusting machine, a cylindrical tumbler, where rugs take an hour-long beating until all the dry dirt gets knocked out of them. They get vacuumed and dye tested. Next stop is the wash pit, which is like a soapy waterslide for rugs. They get soaped and thoroughly rinsed with pressurized water, before heading to the centrifuge, where wet rugs get rolled onto a long bar and inserted into a giant tube that spins, driving out the moisture. And last, rugs get hung out to dry on hanging racks, where they get hit on all sides with massive fans.

The best candidates for rug washing are high-quality rugs made of natural fibers. Sisal rugs cannot be washed, and rugs made of viscose, a synthetic fiber, can be tricky to clean because the process can turn them brown.

Summary: Choosing Your Rug

- Search for hand-knotted as opposed to machine-made.

- Opt for natural fiber (wool on cotton) and natural dyes.

- Know that the thinner the rug, the better and the higher the knots per inch.

- Try it in your home before committing.

- Be sure you love it.

CHAPTER 28

Getting Upholstered Furniture Right

B uying a sofa or sectional is likely the biggest furniture decision you will make. Big as in it takes up a lot of space. Big as in if you make a mistake, there's no hiding it behind a potted plant.

Sofas or sectionals (two or more upholstered seating components that go together) are arguably the most used and abused pieces of furniture in the house. I remember the paralysis that set in when I was choosing ours.

Two sofas? Sofa and two chairs? Sofa and love seat? Sectional? Which way should they face? And what about arms, legs, cushions, fill?

I called Bondi Coley, spokeswoman for Lee Industries, a wholesale manufacturer of upholstered furniture, for some couch therapy. The North Carolina–based company has been making furniture since 1969, so they have this stuff down.

"A great sofa or sectional is like a member of the family," said Coley. "It provides the opportunity for togetherness. It's where the kids, grandkids, dogs, grown-ups, all crash out and watch Netflix."

Coley speaks from experience. Her own blue-denim sectional survived her two now-grown boys, their two Labs, and a regular dogpile of friends and still looks good.

"Our typical customer is fifty to sixty years old. They are landing in the home where they plan to stay."

If you're rightsizing, this means you.

Staying is key, because a custom-sized sofa or sectional is just that, tailored to a space. Unlike coffee or end tables, these big items don't always transition well to the next home.

But if you have found or are already living in the rightsized home where you plan to stay, a well-designed sofa set or sectional can help the room cohere in a way that unmatched pieces of furniture can't.

The Eight F's of Finding Furniture

Because living areas get heavy, not just occasional, use, look for well-made products from manufacturers who have been around a while, and that don't skimp. They use hard wood, eight-way, hand-tied springs, and high-quality fill. Here's what else to consider when making that big decision:

1. **Focal point.** Map out how the furniture will sit in the room. Make a to-scale drawing of your room on graph paper. Indicate windows, doors, and traffic flow to determine shape and size. Play with various combinations of sofas, love seats, chairs, or a sectional. Some furniture stores offer paper cutouts of pieces, so you can see how the furniture will fit in your home. The

arrangement shouldn't block a doorway, obstruct a sight line, or, if against a window, stick up higher than the window ledge. Consider traffic flow and focal point. If the focal point is a television, be sure every seat can see it. Try floating the furniture off the walls. Mark off the area on the floor with masking tape to visualize how the pieces will fit.

2. **Fit.** Measure twice, order once. Measure every dimension. Consider delivery dimensions, too. The pieces might fit in the room all right, but be sure they can get in the door, around the corner, and up the stairs.

3. **Fannies.** How many people do you want to seat? A sofa and love seat can comfortably seat five people, while a sectional covering the same area can seat seven or eight, so it can save space and eliminate the need to buy multiple sofas and chairs.

4. **Fashion.** When picking any upholstered piece, style is the first focus. Do you want arms straight or curved, a tight back or loose-back cushions, legs visible or skirted? Find your look.

5. **Frame.** Test the sturdiness of a frame by picking up one leg of a sofa. If the other three legs stay on the ground, that's a problem. A hardwood frame, which you want, won't bend. When you lift a corner, the whole sofa comes with it. When testing out a chair, sit in it and scooch your hips back and forth. The chair should sit tight. Eight-way, hand-tied springs are also the gold standard.

6. **Fabric.** Levels of fabric affect price. When comparing swatches, don't just look at color. Assess durability.

Look at the content and feel the fabric to make sure it has what designers call a nice hand. Hold the fabric up to the light. You shouldn't see through it. Fine linen is lovely, but you don't want it on a sofa you use often. Inquire about "rubs," a durability rating. A machine tests the fabric for wear by literally rubbing it back and forth thousands of times. Fabric that holds up to more than 15,000 rubs is heavy-duty. If you have pets that get on your furniture, avoid any fabric with a loop that a pet can snag and pull with its claws. You might also consider getting a fabric that is the same color as your pet's fur.

7. **Fill.** All-foam cushions are the most basic. They have a harder sit and will break down faster than other fills. Seat cushions with innerspring coils wrapped in foam will last longer. For a sofa you want to collapse onto every day, innerspring seat cushions wrapped in foam and then in feather down or down alternative may be your personal cloud. Like choosing a mattress, the best way to know what you like is to try it.

8. **Features.** Depending on your lifestyle, you can order chairs, sofas, and sectionals that recline (nice for theater rooms) or roll out to make sleepers. You can also opt for furniture with slipcovers, which you can remove and wash or change with the season.

Caring for Upholstered Furniture

John Gartner, a professional upholstery cleaner and owner of Major Floor Care, a cleaning company based in Altamonte

Springs, Florida, is, unfortunately, a regular at my house. His records show he's been to my home five times in as many years. "That's pretty typical of houses with kids or pets," he says, which makes me feel only a slightly better.

I call him when the surface soil around the house hits my tipping point, or when we have a pet emergency, like when our sixty-pound rescue hound Luke (aka Marmaluke, Luclear War, Luk-o-motion) expresses himself, or Pippin, our miniature Labradoodle, has wiped his muzzle, followed by his entire body, along the length of the white sectional, one too many times.

"Typically, homes get dirty gradually, so owners don't notice," said Gartner, who has been cleaning furniture and carpet for twenty-six years. "They call when they hit a pain point, like they have company coming."

Nothing fazes him. He's seen and cleaned stains from every substance you can imagine and some you can't: chocolate, coffee, grease, ink, lipstick, blood, barf, red wine, nail polish, urine, diaper failures, and all-around surface soil. But pets and kids keep upholstery and carpet cleaners in business, he said.

In addition to know-how and having the right chemicals on his truck, companies like his also have the right equipment, including a DriMaster tool, which looks like a squeegee attached to a hose. The business end pressure-injects water and cleaning solution into the fabric through one channel and simultaneously vacuum-sucks the moisture back out through another, so furniture gets cleaned and not soaked, which can leave watermarks.

Before you call a pro, here are tips for treating soiled furniture yourself. The first rule is to act fast. Don't let stains sit. The quicker a stain gets treated, the greater the chances it will come out. After thirty days, it may be too late. Always blot, never rub. Whether on upholstery, rugs, or carpet, rubbing will grind the substance in and wear down the fibers, possibly making the stain permanent. And always use cold water. Hot water sets stains fast. Club soda is often a good start.

You can treat many pet stains with a mild solution of half white vinegar, half water, and a few drops of dishwashing soap. (Vinegar loosens urine from fibers, Gartner said.) Pour a small amount of solution on the stain. Let it sit for several minutes and then blot it with a white towel. Use a fan to dry. Depending on the fabric (test on a hidden area first), a small amount of household hydrogen peroxide can also lift some stains like red wine and coffee. On greasy stains, citrus-based cleaners work well because they break down oil.

Go easy on the soap. A few drops are enough. Too much cleaning solution might get the stain out but will leave a soapy residue that will attract dirt and cause the area to get dirty again.

When you have more than a few light spots to touch up or a heavily soiled item, call a professional. "If there's vomit involved, carefully scrape up what you can, then don't touch it. Have a pro come out," Gartner said.

Clearly, we could talk about many more types of household goods. Although the previous chapters have hit the highlights of what goes in the major rooms of a home, the items covered are not exhaustive. But I hope you get the idea. The act of learning what makes a basic household item excel at its job is a habit you can continue to develop, so you buy your household items right the first time and don't buy more than you need.

It's a worthy pursuit.

The Art of Living

Although I don't think of myself as a snob, I understand that someone reading the previous installments about hand-made rugs, French-milled soap, bougie bedding, crystal wineglasses, and custom sofas might think otherwise.

This makes me wonder, how did I, the product of a very middle-class family, public schools, trailer vacations, and casserole dinners, get so fussy? When did some of the finer things in life go from being for other people to *I can't live without them?*

Awareness is the culprit. Once you discover the difference between polyester sheets and pure cotton, or a thick-rimmed and a thin-rimmed wineglass, or grocery store bar soap and triple-milled, anything less feels like a demotion. And while ignorance may be blissfully cheaper, appreciating the finer things in life does not always come at a price.

MARNI MANTRA:
A small amount of
great beats a lot
of mediocre.

I once heard a woman say, "I am too poor to buy cheap clothes. I need them to last, so I save up." That's true for household furnishings, too. You need to be a discerning consumer. Luxury gets a bad rap. Which brings me to one more mantra: *A small amount of great beats a lot of mediocre.*

Ultimately, living well in your rightsized home means not only furnishing it with the fewest, best-performing household goods possible but also having just enough house—not too much, not too little—in just the right place.

Now that you've read this book, you should be able to answer for yourself the question of where you should live to realize your best life and in how much house. You should also have a better understanding of the difference between living and living well.

One is merely existing; the other is an art.

A rightsized life is part of the art of living. As we've seen, it doesn't just happen. Rather, it requires honesty, courage, determination, editing, and intention. At the heart of every rightsizing journey lies the desire to evolve, to become better, to live better.

I hope you'll start your rightsizing journey today. Envision where you want to live and how. Then clean house, mentally and physically. Work through the fears, the excuses, the inertia, the literal stuff, and all that stands between you and your best life.

Then get moving. Live where you belong. And get the good soap.

Live well,

Marni

EPILOGUE

Where Are They Now?

A *s this book went to press, I circled back to find out how some of the sources we met along the way were doing on their right-sizing journey. Here's where they are:*

Andy Fine is still in his Bay Area home mulling his options, which he's largely narrowed to staying in the area (though possibly in a smaller home) or moving to Iowa. He plans to visit his son and family there over the holidays to test the waters.

Craig and Chiqeeta Jameson had just finished unloading their moving truck and were settling into their new home in Midland, Michigan. The home is 30 percent larger and 60 percent less expensive than their former home in Los Angeles. In the first week, Craig discovered and attended a gathering of the Midland Classical Guitar Association, which meets twice a month.

Liz Hicks is also where we left her, but by intention not default. The rightsizing exercise caused her to reconsider and better appreciate what she had. She decided, based on what mattered to her (family, friends, and church) that maybe the grass wasn't greener, that maybe moving wasn't the answer. "Seeing the scores so close was helpful for me to find contentment where I am," she wrote in an e-mail.

Katie and Thad Seymour are happily free of their big family home and dividing their time between their two smaller homes, one in Wisconsin near their new granddaughter, and the other in their hometown of Orlando, a lock-up-and-go residence.

In February 2023, less than a year after we spoke, **Howard Bragman,** the fixer with a fixer, passed away unexpectedly from complications of leukemia. He was sixty-six.

Bob Thacker and Karen Cherewatuk have parlayed their love of creating a tailor-made forever home into making the dream of owning a home a reality for a deserving but marginalized family. The couple bought a 130-year-old dilapidated home in Northfield, Minnesota, then rallied their community who donated time, expertise, and materials, and worked alongside the family of five to renovate it. The family moved in August of 2023 and are making payments on the home they plan to pass down for generations.

Bob Glockler has made some changes in his apartment to make it "more about me," he said in an e-mail. He's emptied out his late wife's closet and made it his, has moved some furniture around, and replaced old photos with new ones. And he has found a new companion, a widow who lost her husband in 2021, just a few months before Bob lost his wife. They've been traveling a lot together, hence the new photos. Though she keeps her own apartment, he said, "We have become very close, with the full support of both our families."

Life is happening now. Live with intention.

RESOURCES

America's Test Kitchen
americastestkitchen.com

Artifcts
artifcts.com

Better Sleep Council
bettersleep.org

CraftJack Report
"States Americans are Moving to and From" craftjack.com/toolbox
/states-americans-are-moving-to-and-from

National Association of Productivity and Organizing
napo.net

National Association of Realtors
nar.realtor

**National Association of Realtors' 2023 Home Buyers and Sellers
Generational Trends Report**
https://www.nar.realtor/sites/default/files/documents/2023-home
-buyers-and-sellers-generational-trends-report-03-28-2023.pdf

National Association of Senior Move Managers

nasmm.org

World Population Review 2023 Survey: Cost of Living by State

https://worldpopulationreview.com/state-rankings/cost
-of-living-index-by-state

INDEX

best life, your, 5–6
Better Sleep Council, 176, 191, 233
Boll & Branch, 182, 202

C

change, fear of, 6, 11, 82
climate, 16, 17, 23, 35, 36
closet, clothes,
 hanger management and,
  196–198
 reorganizing your, 195
communities, senior, 21, 59, 60,
 108, 113
complacency, 82
condo(s), 21, 25,
Conran, Terence, 134–137
control, taking, 9
cookware. See pots and pans
cost of living, 17, 37, 38
 by state, 45, 230
CraftJack Report, 16, 233
cutlery. See flatware

D

death, 19, 112
decision tree, stay-or-go, 32–33
decluttering, 58
 course, online, 131
 and downsizing, 64, 66
 importance of, 62, 75
 twelve ways for cleaning and,
  60–64
default, living by, 9
denial, 81
dependent living, 2
Design Museum of London, 134.
 See also Conran, Terence
designer, professional, 90
dining room, 8, 76, 83–84
 unused, 30

disagreements, couples', 107–110
divorce, 19, 49, 87, 93
downsize/downsizing, 8
 decluttering and, 64, 66
 hoarding and, 65
 motivation for, 66
 moving and, 17, 19–20
 reluctance to, 122–124
 retirees and, 20
 seen as rightsizing, 20
dreams, power of, 8–9

E

education
 adult, 23, 24, 37
 age, and political party, 53
 and culture, 37, 39
elevator
 home, 98, 99, 100
 shaftless, 98
 See also stair lift
empty nesters', 2, 67, 72
 reasons to stay in family home,
  81–82
 rightsized dreamhouse, 81–85

F

faith, 11, 71, 131
family history, 8, 61
fate, 11
fear, 82
 of missing out. See FOMO
flatware
 caring for your, 151
 how to pick good, 148–150
 importance of, 147–148
focus, 51, 66, 131
 and direction, 11
 on the pluses, 63–64
 on the upside, 75

ABOUT THE AUTHOR

Marni Jameson is a nationally syndicated home and lifestyle columnist, award-winning journalist, speaker, frequent television guest, and author of six bestselling books, including *What to Do with Everything You Own to Leave the Legacy You Want* and *Downsizing the Family Home*. Her humorous and helpful weekly column on all things home appears in newspapers nationwide reaching several million readers. A longtime reporter for Tribune Media, including the *Los Angeles Times* and *Orlando Sentinel*, she has also written for such top-tier media as *Forbes, Woman's Day*, and *Family Circle*. The mother of a blended family of five grown children, Marni lives in Winter Park, Florida, with her husband, DC, and their two unruly dogs.